THE EFFECTIVE INTERPRETING SERIES

Cognitive Processing in ASL

Carol J. Patrie, Ph.D.

DawnSignPress

San Diego, California

The Effective Interpreting Series: Cognitive Processing in ASL

Producer: Joe W. Dannis

Printed in the United States of America

Published by DawnSignPress

Rosetta Stone image © Copyright The British Museum. The Rosetta Stone appears throughout the series as a symbol of translation's importance to mankind. The basalt slab was discovered in July 1799 in the small Egyptian village of Rosette on the western delta of the Nile. The stone's inscription in hieroglyphic, demotic, and Greek languages led to a crucial breakthrough in research regarding Egyptian hieroglyphs. This key to "translating silent images" into a living language symbolizes the importance of accurate transmissions of messages from one language into another.

The Rosetta Stone now resides in the British Museum in London.

Cover Design: Greg Smith

ISBN-13: 978-158121-113-9

10   9   8   7   6   5   4   3   2   1

ATTENTION: SCHOOL AND DISTRIBUTORS

Quantity discounts for schools and bookstores are available.
For information, please contact:

DÄWNSIGNPRESS

6130 Nancy Ridge Drive
San Diego, CA 92121-3223
(858) 625-0600 V • (858) 625-2336 Fax

Visit us at www.dawnsign.com

For Joe Dannis with deepest gratitude
for his generosity and commitment to my work.
May his path always be made smooth and filled with Light.

Acknowledgments

The inspiration for this book and all of the books in *The Effective Interpreting Series* was granted to me in a flash one evening in 1994. I was fortunate that Providence led me to Joe Dannis and DawnSignPress. We have been working together on these materials since 1995. I am grateful to Joe and his unwavering commitment to my creativity. He has had both courage and generosity to support this long-term and ongoing project with all its unexpected twists and turns. He is the steady hand in the background behind *The Effective Interpreting Series*.

As an author it is my privilege and honor to acknowledge all those who have assisted in the development and production of this book. I experience gratitude again as I realize that many people at DawnSignPress worked diligently and patiently over time to bring this book to publication. I thank each of the people at DawnSignPress within the following departments; accounting, customer service, marketing and warehouse. Many DSP staffers also serve dual roles by working at conventions and in various other ways behind the scenes. Creating one book truly takes the dedication of many. I offer special thanks to Joe Seifrid for his enthusiasm about *The Effective Interpreting Series* and his continuing attention to marketing this product in creative ways.

One of the hallmarks of DawnSignPress products is high quality DVDs. I am indebted to Laura Harvey for her superb skills in video editing and to Matt Ellis for his painstaking work on video captures. I thank all those involved in filming and video editing including, Yoon Lee, Eric Calbert, and Susan Jones. A special thanks to Matt Ellis, who coordinated the book layout and printing of the books, and did painstaking work on the video captures for print.

I thank all the speakers who took time from their busy schedules to be videotaped for this project. Special thanks go to Anne Marie Baer, Ben Bahan, Barbara Buchanan, Brooke Budzinski, Elizabeth Creamer, Matt Ellis, Quintin Greenfield, Vaughn Hallada, C. J. Jones, Missy Keast, Troy Kotsur, Ayuk Ogork, Jessica Olsen-Dunbar, Steve Sandy, and Minnie Mae Wilding-Diaz.

I am grateful to Daniel Gile for his elegant Effort Models, fascinating discussions, and for sharing insight into his work. Brenda Nicodemus was kind enough to offer her comments regarding prosody in ASL, which were very helpful to me.

I offer continual respect and gratitude to Rebecca Ryan who has carefully guided all seven books *The Effective Interpreting Series* from first draft to publication. This is a huge feat and she has undertaken the development and editing of each volume with insight and precision. She is a role model and source of inspiration for me in her selfless dedication to *The Effective Interpreting Series*.

I am deeply grateful for the tremendous amount of positive feedback on previous volumes in *The Effective Interpreting Series* from teachers, students, and interpreters. It is a privilege to bring you the seventh volume in the series. I hope you will enjoy it and I look forward to your valuable feedback.

Contents

Preface

When I became a professional interpreter in 1968, interpreter education was rare. Since that time, interpreter education has made great strides. Soon after my first year of professional interpreting in 1968, I began attempting to teach interpreting. From that time to now, I have been building a store of ideas and materials related to teaching interpretation. I am pleased to share with you my 38 years of experience. I am one of the developers of the Master of Arts in Interpretation at Gallaudet University, where I taught interpretation from 1984 to 2000. I am now the Director of Curriculum and Instruction for The Effective Interpreting Professional Education Series at Language Matters, Inc. I am enthusiastic about developing interpreter education materials and providing up-to-date training for interpreters and interpreter educators and welcome your feedback on this and other volumes in the series.

See www.language-matters.com for additional information on credit courses offered by Language Matters that address the topics in *The Effective Interpreting Series*. LMI also offers graduate level courses on teaching interpreting.

The exercises presented in this book result from my desire to develop materials practicing and future interpreters can use in or out of the classroom while studying simultaneous interpretation. This book can be used independently of any other book in *The Effective Interpreting Series,* or it can be used as one of the sequence of five books that provide a systematic approach to developing skills in simultaneous interpreting from ASL.

In my experience I have found that one of the greatest challenges in interpreter education for signed or spoken language is finding or creating appropriate materials for use in the classroom. An even more severe problem is overcoming the lack of study materials that practicing and future interpreters can use on their own, either for refresher practice or for continuing professional development. There is a growing demand for mentorship in both signed and spoken language interpretation and materials to optimize these contacts.

Simultaneous interpreting is a very complex skill that requires intensive and appropriate practice. It is my hope that by providing materials for developing interpreting skills from ASL, practicing and future interpreters will find the process of developing interpretation skills to be rewarding and effective.

Successful interpreters rely on many skills in their everyday work. The development of these skills is not intuitive or automatic. Simultaneous interpreting must be developed through a careful sequence of learning activities. Isolating specific skills and learning them one at a time is the best approach to learning complex new skills. Learning new skills one at a time allows mastery of individual skills and a feeling of success. Gaining control over components of the interpretation process can assist in developing simultaneous interpreting skills because appropriate practice helps to routinize these complex skills. The skills that make up the simultaneous interpreting processes are generally not used in isolation and must be synthesized correctly in order to render an interpretation.

Component skills for simultaneous interpreting are interactive and interdependent. The learning process should begin with strengthening skills in your first language (L1) and move in a carefully structured sequence from intralingual skill development to *inter*lingual development. The first five volumes in *The Effective Interpreting Series* provide English source materials and exercises that focus on cognitive processing, English skills development, translation, and consecutive and simultaneous interpreting. This volume, the first in the ASL series, provides practice materials designed to enhance ASL skills needed for ASL-English interpretation.

Description of the Materials

This set of materials includes a teacher's guide and a student study set. The teacher's guide includes all of the information in the student study set plus instructions for the teacher. The books refer to the exercises on the DVD. What makes this volume unique is that you will answer the study questions in ASL. The ASL intralingual skills in this study set focus on comprehension, memory, repetition, and pattern inference. Throughout the entire volume there is a strong emphasis on developing reliable comprehension skills because comprehension forms the basis for faithful interpretations.

The DVD

The DVD contains video segments that are to be used with the book. The directions for each exercise tell you when to watch the DVD and how to provide your answers. The DVD has been designed to offer access to the video segments that correspond to the specific exercises and questions.

The DVD opens with a list of all units.

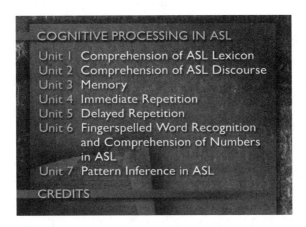

After choosing a unit, you then choose which exercise.

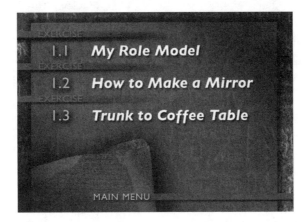

The exercise menus guide you to the specific segment you need to complete the exercise. Each exercise has clips where signers tell a story, or give sentence level information in ASL.

Here is an example of the exercise menu.

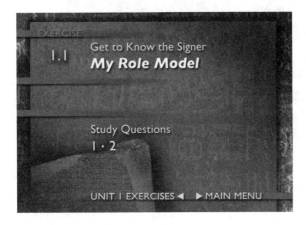

Not all exercises have all types of segments, but here is an explanation of the possible parts of each exercise.

Get to Know the Signer

Some exercises have a short segment where the signer introduces himself or herself. There are comprehension questions related to these segments. The story titles are used as the title of the exercise.

Main Selection

In each exercise the signer tells a story or gives information in ASL. That is the white title at the top of each exercise menu.

Study Questions and Comprehension Questions

This part is where you answer questions regarding the signer's story, or regarding your performance of the exercise. If the book shows a video capture, there will be a segment on the DVD to help you answer that question.

The short clips that relate to study or comprehension questions are broken down at sentence or idea level. There are times when one clip includes information for several questions. In these instances, the numbers for the questions are grouped together. After each study or comprehension question clip is done playing, the DVD returns you to the exercise menu and highlights the clip you have just seen. This functions as "play again." If you wish to view the clip several times, simply play the clip again at the menu. If you are done answering the questions related to a clip, use your DVD remote or the controls for your DVD software to select the next question or group of questions to continue.

In the book, the questions with a related clip include a video capture and time code to help you focus on the exact part of the video needed to answer the question.

01:00:40;20

At the bottom of the screen in every exercise menu, the DVD has a link to the unit exercises, and the main menu.

Introduction to Cognitive Processing Skills in ASL

The Importance of ASL Language Skills for Interpreters

This study set focuses on development of cognitive processing skills within ASL. Many authors have written about the importance of language competence in interpreter education. When skills are developed *within* a language, these skills are called *intralingual*. When the skills are mastered and effectively used, then language competence is present. In developing mastery of intralingual skills, it is best to begin in one's first language (L1), with eventual practice in one's second language (L2). Roberts, (1992) says, "Language competency, which covers the ability to manipulate with ease and accuracy the *two* languages involved in the interpreting process, is a prerequisite for successful interpreting of a message, for the message is mediated through language" (p. 1, emphasis added). She further subdivides the idea of language competency by saying language competency includes the "ability to understand the source language in all its nuances and the ability to express oneself correctly, fluently, clearly and with poise in the target language" (Roberts, p. 2). It is clear that high levels of competency are required in both languages to ensure faithful interpretations.

Intralingual skills must be well developed in both languages used in the interpreting process. When intralingual skills are well developed, the amount of effort needed for processing information is reduced. Because simultaneous interpreting is a very difficult task, it is best to reduce the amount of effort needed by mastering the component skills before combining them into the more cognitively complex skills needed for simultaneous interpreting.

Moser (1983) suggests that competence in monolingual exercises, or exercises within one language, can be a predictor for determining success in interpreter training (p. 43). Arjona (1984) says,

The complexity of the communication process in which a translation or interpretation practitioner must function requires nothing less than superior mastery of the language systems involved. Anything less jeopardizes the standards of performance which of necessity must be professionally assured" (p. 3).

Arjona (1984) suggests that the goal of interpreter training programs is to allow graduates to function with a "minimum competency, proficiency and mastery level needed to perform successfully in real life situations" (p. 3). She explains that the term minimum competency does not mean rock bottom. She uses minimum competency to mean being able to meet the minimum requirement for mastering the task. She goes on to say that candidates for graduation from an interpreter education program must be able to "routinely translate or interpret the message accurately and appropriately, thus bridging the communication gap in a meaningful manner" (p. 6). This means that each individual graduating from a program must be able to perform well against standards for entry to the profession.

What Are Cognitive Processing Skills?

Cognitive processing is the term I use to describe some of the invisible mental processes that are essential to the interpreting process. These mental processes include comprehension, memory, immediate repetition, delayed repetition, recognizing numbers, and pattern inference. Each of these terms is explained. Accompanying exercises within the units that follow allow you to practice each skill. It is essential to have these basic processing mechanisms under control to support other skills in the interpreting process. The interpreter must be able to process linguistically complex material as quickly and efficiently as possible. Gonzalez et al. (1991) point out that the routinization of complex tasks such as those listed here can reduce the amount of conscious effort needed for the interpreting process. These authors go on to say that the complicated skills in the interpreting process can be positively affected by training. When complex tasks become more routine, the interpreter's attention can be focused on more demanding tasks such as register and stylistic issues. These authors remind us that multiple tasks must occur simultaneously during the interpreting process.

Why Develop Cognitive Processing Skills?

Successful interpreters have many skills that they rely on in their everyday work. Quick access to cognitive processing skills underlies many of the more complicated aspects of the interpreting process. This means that interpreters must be able to quickly make sense out of what they see and hear and decide what the message means and how to transfer that message into another language with split-second accuracy. Shreve and Koby (1997) point out that during the past 25 years, there has been much interest in trying to describe the cognitive processes associated with interpreting. They contend that these mental operations are largely "hidden," yet form a complex and essential part of the interpreting process.

The systematic development of the cognitive processing skills that underlie the interpreting process is very important. If cognitive processing skills are not developed and available, then there is a much higher chance that the skills that must be developed later, such as translation, consecutive interpreting, and simultaneous interpreting, will not be strongly grounded and may be more difficult to master. A deficit in cognitive processing skills could result in interpretations that are skewed or contain errors. Specific cognitive processing skill deficits can lead to particular types of errors in interpreting. For example, we may find that a relationship exists among poor auditory memory, short lag time, and an increase in overall errors (Cokely, 1992a). The development of cognitive processing skills can reduce the amount of effortful processing that is required to perform a successful simultaneous interpreting.

Gile (1997) indicates that even the performance of practicing interpreters who enjoy excellent professional reputations can contain errors such as wrong numbers, wrong names, or wrong propositional content and that these errors can occur up to several times per minute. He goes on to explain that these errors can occur even under the best working conditions. The interpreters he refers to do not have apparent "weaknesses in terms of the source language or target language proficiency, world knowledge or interpreting skills" (p. 197). Gile suggests there is an intrinsic difficulty in interpreting and that the difficulty lies in the cognitive processing tasks involved and describes the three efforts that make up his Effort Model of Interpreting (1995). According to Gile the three efforts are Listening and Analysis, Production and the Short Term Memory Effort. During the interpreting process, the interpreter distributes effort among these three areas. In practicing the skills in this study set, you will learn about the importance of being aware of how much effort you are using during the interpreting process. By practicing isolated skills in advance of interpreting, you can maximize your use of effort. More detail on Gile's Effort Model is included below.

These materials provide a clear approach to developing cognitive processing skills in ASL as they relate to simultaneous interpreting. An emphasis is placed on analyzing cognitive processing skills by providing exercises and study questions that give insight into strategies for further developing these essential skills.

The Goal of This Study Set and DVD

The purpose of the study set and accompanying DVD is to improve and enhance your skills in processing ASL before you attempt to interpret from or to ASL. It is important to develop ASL skills with conscious effort, even if ASL is your first language. You may not have had the opportunity before now to study ASL as it relates to the interpreting process if ASL is your second language. This study set provides you with specific skills that will build confidence in your ASL skills. As you use this study set, your ASL skills and awareness of the importance of these skills improve.

Seven important ASL skills are presented in this study set. These ASL skills are separated into seven units in the study set for two reasons. First, ineffective results commonly are achieved when anyone attempts to learn the interpreting process as a whole and has no prior experience in interpreting. The second reason for separating the eight skills is the easy identification of problem areas. Separating the component skills allows you to experience mastery of the components of the larger process.

Models of the Interpreting Process

There are many different ways to describe the interpreting process. No two are exactly alike, but all models of the process indicate that interpretation is a multistage process. Moser (1997) summarizes some of the better known models of interpreting. She mentions the following models: Gerver (1976), Moser-Mercer (1978), Kitano (1993), Pradis (1994), and a summary of Daro and Fabbro's (1994) model of memory during interpreting.

Moser indicates that many models use an information processing approach to explain the interpreting process. Information systems models are based on computer-style operations. This kind of analysis will be necessarily somewhat flawed because human minds do not operate exactly as computers do. Nevertheless, models provide a way to talk about the complex process of interpreting. Another point that Moser makes is that even though most researchers will agree that interpreting is a multistage process, they do not agree on the names of the stages or the contents of the stages or even how many there are. Moser states that "A powerful model of the interpreting process must be broad enough to include aspects that reflect the complex, time constrained multitasking environment of simultaneous interpreting that involves a high degree of cognitive processing" (1997, p. 194). For detailed information on the models mentioned, please refer to the chapter by Moser in Danks (1997).

In this study set, I emphasize Gile's (1995) Effort Model because it provides a clear and simple framework for the importance of cognitive processing tasks. The Effort Model provides a powerful explanation for the importance of developing intralingual skills before learning the interpreting process. The model shows that processing capacity for interpreting is available in limited supply and is not automatic.

Gile (1995) suggests that there are three main effort areas in the interpreting process. The first is the Listen and Analysis Effort, which deals with comprehension, the Production Effort, which includes speech planning and verbal output, and the Memory Effort, which deals with the stresses placed on the short-term memory system. The Coordination Effort integrates these three efforts. Gile also suggests that each interpreter has certain capacities within each of these areas of effort. Ideally, the interpreter has more capacity than is required by a given interpreting task.

Regardless of which model of interpreting you choose to study, you will soon see that all models require that the incoming message be analyzed and understood before any part of the transfer process can begin, so these materials emphasize that area of effort.

When to Learn Cognitive Processing Skills?

If you are a novice or new interpreter, cognitive processing skills should be developed before moving on to more advanced skills, which compose the interpreting process. If you are beyond the beginning stages of an interpreter education program or are already an experienced interpreter, you can also benefit from practice in cognitive processing skills, either as a refresher course or for professional skills maintenance.

Experienced interpreters who are now working may not have had the benefit of studying the individual skills that make up the interpreting process. Experienced interpreters often search for specific ways to improve their interpreting skills. Practice on the components of the interpreting process, such as cognitive processing skills, can be meaningful and productive practice for experienced interpreters who wish to work independently on skills improvement. Strong and quick cognitive processing skills form a good basis on which to develop or practice more complex skills in the interpreting process.

When students in interpreter education programs experience a plateau effect in training, that point at which skills appear to be no longer developing as rapidly as they did earlier in the training process, it is often useful to go back to an earlier stage of skills development and practice at that earlier level. Taking time to go back and review skills is a positive step because it increases confidence, builds mastery, and often provides the springboard to further progress.

Specific Cognitive Processing Skills

It is important for professionals in the field of interpreting to use meaningful and precise language in discussing their work. To update our professional language, it may be necessary to examine the terminology used in the past and determine whether it is accurate, transparent and meaningful. Language professionals have a clear obligation to use accurate language in discussing their work.

In this study set, terms that are as transparent and as accurate as possible will be used to promote a clearer understanding of the processes involved. In earlier phases of our profession, the following terms have been used to refer to the cognitive processing skills that form part of the interpreting process: shadowing, prediction, and cloze. These terms have been borrowed from cognitive psychology and reading proficiency and in their truest definitions are somewhat misleading if we apply them directly to the interpreting process. The term "shadowing" has been used, but in fact the process is *repetition*. The term "prediction" has been widely used in the interpreter education field to encompass the process of completing sentences or ideas. In actuality, prediction means to make known in advance on the basis of special knowledge; to foretell or prophesy. These connotations contradict many of the central tenets of the interpreting process. Interpreters may reasonably be expected to infer what information would logically fit in the given context, but not simply to guess or imagine without a reasoned basis. The term "cloze" has been borrowed from the field of language acquisition and was originally intended as a measure of language proficiency in reading. Although reading proficiency may indicate high levels of overall language proficiency, in interpreting we are most interested in high levels of using language to communicate in real time. The broader, more accurate term of pattern inference is used in this study set in keeping with providing clear and accurate professional language.

Terminology

Here are some other basic terms and their meanings as they are used in this study set:

Comprehension

The American Heritage Dictionary defines comprehension as taking in the meaning or importance of something, to grasp. Dancette (1997) notes, "To understand a text is to build a meaningful and coherent representation of its conceptual content" (p. 78).

Memory

The American Heritage Dictionary defines memory as the mental capacity of recalling or recognizing previously learned behavior or past experience.

Immediate Repetition

Immediate repetition means to say or perform again without delay. This type of repetition is begun as soon as listeners can begin processing what they have seen. There is no enforced delay in this kind of repetition. This term replaces the formerly used term "shadowing" because immediate repetition is a precise and descriptive term for the activity.

Delayed Repetition

Delayed repetition means to say or perform again with a delay. This type of repetition is characterized by an enforced delay before the repetition process begins. The delay could be either a short time interval or an idea unit. This term replaces the formerly used term of shadowing with delay.

Repetition

Repetition means to sign or say again, without delay, exactly what you are seeing or hearing. The term "shadowing" has been widely used in interpreter education to refer repetition but the term 'shadowing' does not reveal the intent of this cognitive skill clearly. In this text, immediate repetition and delayed repetition are used, rather than shadowing.

Number Repetition

This term is used here to describe the process of repeating speeches that contain numbers. Repetition of selections containing numbers can be done with or without delay.

Pattern Inference

A pattern is defined as a model or original used as an archetype or a model to be followed in making things. Inference means the act of deriving logical conclusions from information known to be true or reasoning from factual knowledge or evidence. Here, two types of pattern inference exercises are presented, word-level pattern inference and phrase-level pattern inference. Pattern inference demonstrates the awareness of usual patterns within a language.

Word-Level Pattern Inference

Word-level pattern inference means to infer a single word that can logically fit in the context provided. This term replaces the formerly used term cloze.

Phrase-Level Pattern Inference

Phrase-level pattern inference refers to the ability to select a phrase that can logically be used in the context provided. This term replaces the formerly used term prediction.

Process and Product

In interpreter education there is always much discussion over whether students should focus on the process of interpreting or the product of the interpretation. My position is that both are equally important and should be part of even the earliest stages of training. It is vital that you understand the difference between these two terms and the role they play in your education and training as an interpreter. The process of interpreting is largely invisible. The process is what goes on in your head as you listen, analyze, transfer the meaning to another language, and find expression for that message in another language. This part of the interpreting event cannot be recorded or observed by another person. Only via introspection can interpreters gain insight into their own process and make changes to it. Gile (1995) suggests that the use of a process-oriented approach can optimize training time. In his opinion, it is best not to focus only on the end products of the translation process, but rather to include information on "principles, methods and procedures" (Gile, p. 10). Gile goes on to support his idea this way:

> By concentrating on the reasons for errors or good choices in translation rather than on the words or structures produced by the students, teachers devote most of their effective teaching time to Translation strategies and lose little time over their by-products. (p. 11)

The product is the observable part of your work. It is the interpretation that the "listener" receives from the "sender" via your interpreting. The product can be recorded for future analysis, whereas the process cannot. Seal (1999) has summarized the results of a recent study of interpreters who wished to improve their skills. In that report, she emphasizes the importance of analyzing one's own work by studying the video taped interpretation. Seal notes,

> Self-analysis, the zenith of any professional development activity, is highly facilitated when we step back and take a look at ourselves. Routine videotaping and observing videotaped performances for strengths and weaknesses and for changes over time is quite possibly the most valuable, yet least frequently accomplished activity we can engage in. (Seal, p. 14)

This study set is designed to assist in the development of specific cognitive processes in the interpreting process. The development of these processes is accomplished through a combination of strategies. The first step is to read the information in each chapter, which provides you with insight into the importance of the process and the product. Next, you actually perform the exercise and record your work. This gives you an opportunity to experience the process and also to create a product. In the next step, you answer the study questions. The answers to the study questions allow you to focus on the product to see whether your work is accurate or needs improvement. By examining your product, redoing the exercises, and studying how the product varies from one try to the next, you gain a deeper insight into how variations on the process that are under your control can affect the product.

How to Use This Book

The cognitive processing skills addressed in this text are comprehension, memory, immediate repetition, delayed repetition, recognizing fingerspelled words and numbers, word-level pattern inference, and phrase-level pattern inference. Throughout, there is an ongoing emphasis on fingerspelled word recognition as an essential component of comprehension. All of the exercises in each unit may be completed as out-of-classroom work, although I recommend that the first exercise in each unit be used as an in-class exercise to become familiar with the goals and tasks in each unit.

For either independent or group work, this study set provides complete directions for each exercise. The directions guide you to the correct location on the accompanying DVD. Each exercise has a combination of comprehension questions and study questions. The study questions provide focus and insight into your responses to the exercises. The study set exercises provide the opportunity to take responsibility not only for creating work, but also for developing strategies for improvement. At the end of each unit there is a progress tracking sheet. Use this sheet to note the date you completed the exercises, to make notes regarding your progress, and to record any questions you may have about the exercise.

What You Will Need before Beginning the Exercises

You will need specific equipment to get the maximum benefit from these exercises: a DVD player with a remote control that will allow pausing and frame advance, a monitor, an audio recorder, video recording device, recording material, a quiet place to work, a copy of the DVD that accompanies this study set, and this study set.

When and Where You Should Plan to Do the Exercises

Each exercise can be done independently. This means that you should either plan to do them out of class on your own time or in a class format if your training program has a place for you to record your work. However, your instructor may conduct some of the exercises in group format. Where you do the exercises will depend on your instructor and the equipment available in your interpreter education program.

If you are a practicing interpreter and want to work on developing your skills, you will still need all of the equipment listed above and may proceed at your own pace. You may want to follow established procedures for obtaining continuing education units for certification maintenance. Also, you may wish to form a forum with other interpreters in which to discuss your skills development work.

How Many Times Should You Do the Exercises?

You can benefit from doing each exercise at least twice. When you do the exercise the first time, the material that you listen to will be "cold," or unfamiliar. The cognitive processes that you are practicing may be new and unfamiliar as well. When you do the exercise the second time, the material will be "warm," or familiar, because you have seen it once before. You will also be more comfortable with the process the second time. It is a good idea to practice the exercises more than once because this type of practice will allow you to experience good control of the process that you are developing.

Progress Tracking Sheet

Use this sheet to track your progress with the exercises you have completed. After performing the exercise and answering the study questions, fill in the tracking sheet. Note the date that you completed the exercise and give an indication of your level of accomplishment. You can use either a quantitative or a qualitative approach to track your progress.

A quantitative approach uses a point scale. Assigning points to linguistic exercises is arbitrary, but in academic environments you may find the point system more suitable than the qualitative approach. Here is an example of a scale you can use to assign points to your work: excellent (no serious errors) = 5 points; good (some errors, but not serious) = 4 points; fair (many errors, some serious) = 3 points; not satisfactory (many errors, most are serious) = 2 points; poor (missed the point of the exercise—must redo) = 1 point.

Each performance and study question can be assigned a point value. A zero indicates that the question was not answered and a 5 indicates a full and complete answer.

Add the scores in each column (not row) and divide by the number of exercises to get a percentage for the first performance, second performance, and study questions. It is important to have separate percentages for each of these columns because the scores represent different skills. Remember that a second performance on the same material is considered practice on warm or familiar material and should be weighted less than the cold or first performance.

A qualitative approach is well suited to those who are studying the material in an independent fashion or those who do not want to attach numbers and percentages to their work. In a qualitative approach, you describe your evaluation of your work rather than assigning numbers. Write down enough information to remind yourself of your level of achievement in the performance of the exercises and study questions.

The sample chart provides examples of how to note your progress using the quantitative or qualitative approach.

Progress Tracking Sheet

This sheet is designed to help you keep track of which exercises you have completed and how well you have done on these exercises. A rating system is presented for you to rate the outcomes of your work on the exercises. After completing each exercise, fill in the tracking sheet. Rate your performance on the exercises by using this scale: excellent (no serious errors) = 5 points; good (some errors, but not serious) = 4 points; fair (many errors, some serious) = 3 points; not satisfactory (many errors, most are serious) = 2 points; poor (missed the point of the exercise—must redo) =1 point.

Exercise Number and Name	Date	First Performance Rating	Second Performance Rating	Questions and Reminders
Exercise 1 My Role Model	1/2	3	2	Fingerspelled word recognition needs attention; study geography
Exercise 2 How to Make a Mirror	9/24	3	4	Need more background knowledge
Exercise 3 Trunk to Coffee Table	9/30	3	4	Need to build endurance; study fs words and terms

UNIT 1

Comprehension of ASL Lexicon

Unit 1 focuses on one important aspect of the interpreting process: comprehension at the lexical level. Interpreters must understand the source material before beginning the interpretating process. Comprehension of the source material is a skill that underlies cognitive processing skills development, as well as the interpretating process as a whole. According to Gile (1995), comprehension is based on two basic features. One is knowledge of words in a language and the other is knowledge of the grammar of a language. He also says that these two basic features are not enough to ensure comprehension. The context in which the words and grammar are used is an essential ingredient in the comprehension process. In Unit 1, ASL comprehension strategies are introduced and improved through guided practice at the lexical or word level, including fingerspelled words.

The comprehension process generally begins with a message in the source language (SL). When this message is sent to a receiver and understood by the receiver, basic communication is thought to have occurred. In reality, this description is much too simple. As Gile points out, each receiver or viewer, in the case of signed languages, has varying levels of prior knowledge of the vocabulary, the grammar, and the context, all of which influence comprehension. The more background information or extralinguistic knowledge (ELK) a person has, the more likely that person is to understand the message as intended by the sender.

Gonzalez et al. (1991) provide a good summary of the role of comprehension in the interpreting process. They suggest that there are three basic parts to this process. The first is that the interpreter is a receptor who hears the message and analyzes it for meaning. The interpreter's prior knowledge and familiarity with the language help the interpreter to reject any irrelevant or nonsensical meanings. The second is that the interpreter breaks up the message into manageable units of information in a process called *segmentation* (Kelly, 1979). This process allows the interpreter to focus on meaning units, regardless of how many words are in the message. In this part of the process, the interpreter analyzes the form carefully and discovers the meaning of the message. In the third step, the interpreter formulates a version of the message in the target language, the language into which the message is interpreted. In all stages of the interpreting process, fidelity will depend on the interpreter's abilities in comprehension, transfer, and reformulation.

Gile (1995) devotes an entire chapter to the importance of comprehension in the interpreting process in his book entitled *Basic Concepts and Models for Interpreter and Translator Training*. One of the points he stresses is that the interpreter's need for ELK never levels off, but rather increases. Next, he stresses the importance of "deliberate and sustained analysis" (Gile, p. 85). This can be likened to an ongoing process of checking probable meanings with the current context to see whether they make sense and whether the probable meanings are likely to be the meanings intended by the speaker. Another important point from Gile's work is that the type of understanding or comprehension that the interpreter must use is not the same as that used by a layperson. The difference is the intensity with which the interpreter must constantly attend to and analyze the incoming message.

With regard to comprehension difficulties in ASL as they relate to interpreting, Taylor (2002) notes,

> Current research shows a continuing and significant gap in interpreter's ability to comprehend ASL. This basic problem is present prior to any difficulty with the interpretation process itself. The ASL input, the source message, is not understood completely and thus the interpretation has no chance of being successful regardless of the interpreter's processing ability. The literature reports that if interpreters do not understand the source language they cannot possibly interpret the message into a target language (p. 2).

As Taylor (2002) points out, many ASL–English interpretation programs do not require fluency in both ASL and English at entry to the program and so students are faced with trying to master ASL *and* begin their interpretation studies simultaneously. In all other language pairs other than ASL and English, fluency in both languages is required *prior* to interpreter training. The fact that this fluency requirement is not uniformly in place as an entrance requirement for ASL–English interpreting programs leads to unreliable interpreter education outcomes and is the single greatest contributor to the lack of preparedness of graduates to work. Often, program graduates may be able to complete program requirements and not be employment ready. This discrepancy between interpreter education program exit requirements and entry-to-the field requirements is commonly referred to as "the gap." In fact, not only are graduates often not employment ready at program completion, but also they often lack the ASL fluency that should have been in place upon entry into the program. Taylor contends, "The fact is that most graduates of interpreting programs do not have advanced competency in ASL" (p. 3). One way to directly address the shortcoming associated with ASL comprehension is to practice on intralingual exercises in ASL focusing on the lexicon, such as those provided in this unit and in *The Effective Interpreting Series: ASL Skills Development.*

The difficulties associated with ASL comprehension are made more complex by a number of variables. Some of these variables are listed by Taylor (2002) and include ASL sign variation resulting from geographic location, gender, age, and professional status. Interpreters are still required to have high levels of ASL comprehension despite the wide-ranging effects of these variables on the appearance of ASL signs. This is similar to Spanish–English interpreters needing to be able to comprehend a number of variations within Spanish.

Taylor (2002) describes two broad categories of types of language skills. Fundamental language skills are "knowledge-lean" and relate most directly to ASL comprehension at the lexical and discourse levels. In contrast, she describes "knowledge-rich" skills as those that depend on the interpreter's sensitivity to and understanding of the context and language use within that context. Following Taylor's research, we see that errors in ASL comprehension at the fundamental language level fall into the categories of lexicon and discourse errors. Error types within the lexicon include recognition of fingerspelled words, numbers, lexical items (ASL signs), classifiers, nonmanual markers, and negation, among others. Error types within discourse include miscomprehensions of ASL facial grammar above the nose, ASL referencing, spatial relationships, utterance boundaries, recognition of fingerspelled words, and errors related to the signer changing hand dominance. This listing of error types helps define the areas that should receive specific attention during ASL study and practice sessions. Unit 1 also includes a special emphasis on fingerspelled word recognition.

Fingerspelled Word Recognition

Fingerspelled word recognition is central to accurate comprehension of ASL. Accurate fingerspelled word recognition is of particular importance to second language learners who aspire to interact with members of the Deaf community in conversation or in professional contexts. Hearing people who are learning ASL as adults tend to have great difficulty in correctly recognizing fingerspelled words. This specific difficulty often prevents hearing people from becoming truly fluent in ASL and can lead to misunderstandings and frustrations between deaf and hearing people who want to communicate. Problems also occur in the production of fingerspelled words, but these problems tend to be less severe than the problems of fingerspelled word recognition.

Fingerspelled Word Recognition in Interpreting

Interpreting is far more cognitively demanding than simply conversing in ASL. Sign language interpreters may be more acutely aware of the difficulty in correctly recognizing fingerspelled words than other hearing signers because interpreting requires simultaneously managing a wide range of enormously demanding cognitive, linguistic, and interpersonal tasks, including fingerspelled word recognition.

Many interpreters feel that the fingerspelled word recognition process is much more difficult than any other aspect of the interpreting process. When interpreters have trouble understanding fingerspelled words, anxiety increases and often the interpreting process is interrupted.

In contrast, experienced interpreters report that reading fingerspelled words is no different than reading other aspects of sign language and that fingerspelled word recognition is not particularly anxiety producing. The successes of these interpreters must mean that they are using strategies that are appropriate to fingerspelled word recognition. In research studies (Patrie, 1992), novice and expert performances in fingerspelled word recognition were compared. In every comparison, the experienced interpreters performed better than the novice interpreters. We assume that the differences in performance are caused by differences in strategies. The training approaches and information presented in *Rapid Serial Visual Presentation* (Patrie & Johnson, in press) can improve strategies related to the fingerspelled word recognition process.

If you study a fingerspelled word by viewing it at least five times in slow motion, you have a much stronger pattern recognition for that word and are much more likely to recognize that word in the future, even if produced by a different signer. Less time is needed to recognize a fingerspelled word that has been studied previously.

By focusing on comprehension at the lexical and discourse levels through intralingual exercises, you can improve your ASL comprehension and your overall interpreting performance. This unit provides focused practice in comprehension at the lexical level in the context of other salient ASL features.

The comprehension exercises are arranged from easiest to more difficult. Before beginning these exercises, refer back to *How to Use This Book* and go over the list of things you will need before beginning the exercises. Prepare to focus intently on the ASL message by removing as many distractions as you can from your environment so that you can analyze the incoming message accurately and thereby improve comprehension. Think of Gile's (1995) idea of deliberate and sustained analysis as you watch each selection.

EXERCISES IN COMPREHENSION OF ASL LEXICON

EXERCISE 1.1

My Role Model

AYUK OGORK

Directions

This exercise has two selections. This short segment allows you to get to know the signer and become accustomed to his signing style and the second segment allows you to focus on comprehension of his message.

The second selection is approximately 2 minutes long. Watch the selection and answer the study questions in ASL as best as you can. Record your answers in ASL. Watch the selection as many times as you need to fully understand the selection, using slow motion if needed, and answer any remaining study questions. In this exercise you will first identify the ASL feature and then reproduce it. This combination of practice in comprehension and production improves comprehension and use of ASL.

Get to Know the Signer

This short segment allows you to get acquainted with the signer. Watch the selection and replay it until you can answer the following questions. You do not need to record your responses.

1. Where was he born?

   _____

2. How long ago did he move?

   _____

3. Where did he go to school?

   _____

4. What year is he in college and what is his major?

   _____

Study Questions

1. Correct recognition of all fingerspelled words is necessary for complete ASL comprehension. Below, you will find a list of English words that represent the translations of fingerspelled words from this selection. Each word will play at regular speed, in slow motion, and again at regular speed. If a fingerspelled word appeared several times in the selection, it will only appear once here. Play the selected fingerspelled words five times until you are sure you can easily recognize each word.

   After you have studied and can easily recognize each fingerspelled word, turn on your video recording device and spell each fingerspelled word clearly, using it in a sentence. Do not rush through the spelling. Compare your spelling with that of the signer. Note any differences in your productive fingerspelling compared with that of the signer. Practice spelling each word several more times, working to match the signer's spelling.

   English Translations of Fingerspelled Words:

   Model

   Alloy Bibum

   Cameroon

   Washington DC Black Deaf Advocacy (DCBDA)

   Cameroon Deaf Empowerment Organization (CEDO)

2. Use ASL to explain the meaning of the following signs in ASL.

01:00:49;08

01:01:02;09

3. Record yourself signing a list of the main points in this selection.

4. Record yourself signing a summary of this selection in ASL. Compare the main points in your summary with the main points you listed for Question 3. If your summary did not include all the main points you listed in Question 3, record another summary that includes all the main points.

5. Watch the selection again. Now that you have studied the lexical items in the selection, is your overall comprehension improved?

EXERCISE 1.2

How to Make a Mirror
QUINTIN GREENFIELD

Directions

Find this selection on your DVD. This selection is approximately 4 minutes long. Find a quiet place to work where you will not be interrupted while working on this exercise. Be sure you can see the screen clearly. Begin focusing and attend carefully to the signer. After watching the selection, answer the study questions. Record your ASL responses to the study questions.

Study Questions

1. Correct recognition of all fingerspelled words is necessary for complete ASL comprehension. Below you will find a list of English words that represent the translations of fingerspelled words from this selection. Each word will play at regular speed, in slow motion, and again at regular speed. If a fingerspelled word appeared several times in the selection, it will only appear once here. Play the selected fingerspelled words five times until you are sure you can easily recognize each word.

   After you have studied and can easily recognize each fingerspelled word, turn on your video recording device and spell each fingerspelled word clearly, using it in a sentence. Do not rush through the spelling. Compare your spelling with that of the signer. Note any differences in your productive fingerspelling compared with that of the signer. Practice spelling each word several more times, working to match the signer's spelling.

English Translations of Fingerspelled Words:

Quintin Greenfield

High school (HS)

Furniture

Cabinet (spelled cabiet)

Company (CO)

Mirror (spelled mirior)

Smooth

Own

Fix

Square

Make it

Frame

Top

Side

Bottom

Caulk (spelled chlk)

Plastic

Stained (spelled stanid)

Board

Drill

Bulb (spelled blub)

2. Correct recognition of numbers is an essential skill for interpreters. In this clip, several ideas or sentences will show that include a number. Play the selection several times until you can easily recognize each number. After you can easily recognize the numbers, turn on your recording device and sign each number, using it in a new sentence.

1983

4

8

40

3. Who is talking in this segment? Respond in ASL.

01:04:12;03

4. Paraphrase the classifiers in the selection, explaining the meaning without using classifiers. Record yourself repeating those classifiers.

5. Watch the selection again. Now that you have studied the lexical items in the selection, is your overall comprehension improved?

EXERCISE 1.3

Trunk to Coffee Table

ANNE MARIE BAER

Directions

The selection is approximately 7 minutes long. Find a quiet place to work where you will not be interrupted. Be sure you can see the screen clearly. Begin focusing and attending carefully to the signer. After watching the selection, answer the study questions. You will need to record your ASL responses to the study questions.

Study Questions

1. Correct recognition of all fingerspelled words is necessary for complete ASL comprehension. Below, you will find a list of English words that represent the translations of fingerspelled words from this selection. Each word will play at regular speed, in slow motion, and again at regular speed. If a fingerspelled word appeared several times in the selection, it will only appear once here. Play the selected fingerspelled words five times until you are sure you can easily recognize each word.

After you have studied and can easily recognize each fingerspelled word, turn on your video recording device and spell each fingerspelled word clearly, using it in a sentence. Do not rush through the spelling. Compare your spelling with that of the signer. Note any differences in your productive fingerspelling compared with that of the signer. Practice spelling each word several more times, working to match the signer's spelling.

English Translations of Fingerspelled Words:

Anne Marie Baer

Trunk

Buffet

Sofa

Wicker

Joey

Sweaters

Hardware

Common, plywood, scraps

Lid

Extra

Wheel

Trim

Side

Strap, strip

Plaster

Rustic, vanilla

What

2. What was the difficulty with the original lid for the trunk? Record your ASL response.

3. Study this clip until you fully understand all of the classifiers. Then record yourself giving the same information using classifiers. Compare your rendition with that of the signer. Paraphrase sections where you are unsure of classifier use. Review your recording, identifying any changes necessary to improve your rendition of classifiers. Record again.

4. Study this clip until you fully understand all of the classifiers. Then record yourself giving the same information using classifiers. Compare your rendition with that of the signer. Paraphrase sections where you are unsure

of classifier use. Review your recording, identifying any changes necessary to improve your rendition of classifiers. Record again.

5. Study this clip until you fully understand all of the classifiers. Then record yourself giving the same information using classifiers. Compare your rendition with that of the signer. Paraphrase sections where you are unsure of classifier use. Review your recording, identifying any changes necessary to improve your rendition of classifiers. Record again.

6. Study this clip until you fully understand all of the classifiers. Then record yourself giving the same information using classifiers. Compare your rendition with that of the signer. Paraphrase sections where you are unsure of classifier use. Review your recording, identifying any changes necessary to improve your rendition of classifiers. Record again.

7. Study this clip until you fully understand all of the classifiers. Then record yourself giving the same information using classifiers. Compare your rendition with that of the signer. Paraphrase sections where you are unsure of classifier use. Review your recording, identifying any changes necessary to improve your rendition of classifiers. Record again.

8. Study this clip until you fully understand all of the classifiers. Then record yourself giving the same information using classifiers. Compare your rendition with that of the signer. Paraphrase sections where you are unsure of classifier use. Review your recording, identifying any changes necessary to improve your rendition of classifiers. Record again.

9. Watch the selection again. Now that you have studied the lexical items in the selection, is your overall comprehension improved?

Progress Tracking Sheet

This sheet is designed to help you keep track of which exercises you have completed and how well you have done on these exercises. A rating system is presented for you to rate the outcomes of your work on the exercises. After completing each exercise, fill in the tracking sheet. Rate your performance on the exercises using this scale: excellent (no serious errors) = 5 points; good (some errors, but not serious) = 4 points; fair (many errors, some serious) = 3 points; not satisfactory (many errors, most are serious) = 2 points; poor (missed the point of the exercise—must redo) =1 point.

Exercise Number and Name	Date	First Performance Rating	Second Performance Rating	Questions and Reminders
Exercise 1.1 My Role Model				
Exercise 1.2 How to Make a Mirror				
Exercise 1.3 Trunk to Coffee Table				

UNIT 2

Comprehension of ASL Discourse

Unit 1 focused on the importance of comprehension of ASL at the lexical level, placing particular emphasis on fingerspelled word recognition. Unit 2 focuses on the importance of comprehension at the discourse level. Taylor's (2002) research provides evidence that errors in ASL to English interpretation are caused, in part, by errors in ASL comprehension at the lexical and discourse levels. In describing the types of errors associated with comprehension at the discourse level, she emphasizes that the interpreter must understand the syntactic and idiomatic elements of ASL to be able to render an adequate interpretation into English. Taylor says, "Effective interpretation requires a sense of meaning conveyed not only by word choice, but also by phrases, sentences, paragraphs and the entire text. ASL discourse comprehension refers to the ability to grasp and convey this 'big picture' meaning" (p. 69). Unit 2 discusses Taylor's findings and then provides exercises to allow you to improve your comprehension of these important ASL features. Improving your ASL comprehension by careful study of ASL features in natural ASL discourse provides a strong foundation for reliable interpretation skills.

Taylor's (2002) taxonomy of comprehension errors at the discourse level includes seven areas in which she discovered miscomprehensions of ASL. These categories are ASL facial grammar above the nose, referencing, spatial referencing, utterance boundaries, and miscomprehensions resulting from changes in the signer's hand dominance, regional variation in signing, and speed of signing. These fundamental language skills, along with skills at the lexical level, are examples of knowledge-lean skills that are not context sensitive.

One of the general error categories that Taylor (2002) studied was incorrect interpretation of ASL *grammatical facial markers* produced above the nose. Taylor explains that in ASL, facial markers convey questions, emotions, and topicalization. These errors include incorrect interpretation of WH questions ("who?," "what?," and "when?"), yes–no questions, interpreting statements as questions, and confusing emotions with grammar as in the case of a WH question that is signified by a furrowed brow and might be misinterpreted as anger. When a question is signed in ASL, nonmanual markers occur with signs. According to Taylor, "For WH-questions, the eyebrows tend to go down and create a small furrow. Interpreters occasionally perceive this questioning face as an unpleasant emotion and use declarative statement structures as opposed to question structures" (p. 70).

In contrast, raised eyebrows indicate yes–no questions. This marker is sometimes misunderstood as topicalization instead of a question, leading to a misinterpretation. The converse is also possible. Topicalization can be misinterpreted as a yes–no question. Topicalization is used to highlight a point or to indicate the beginning of a new sentence or idea. In English, topicalization is accomplished thorough variations in intonation patterns. There are many other aspects of facial grammar above and below the nose that interpreters should be familiar with and able to understand easily. It is important to remember that "affectual" facial expressions are random and optional, but linguistic facial expressions are grammaticized, fixed, and systematic (Sandler and Lillo-Martin, 2001, p. 28). In the accompanying exercises, you will look for other examples of facial grammar.

The second broad category of errors noted by Taylor (2002) is incorrect interpretation of *ASL referencing*. Referencing is shown in several ways in ASL. Taylor includes the following types of referencing that are discussed in more detail in her research. The signer's *eye gaze* provides information about the person or thing being discussed. *Body orientation* also adds meaning to the message and is often combined with eye gaze. *Indexing* or pointing with the finger also indicates a referent, after it has been established. Signers can change direction of their torso to indicate taking the position of various referents. This has been called "role-shifting" or "characterization." Sometimes the body is moved to convey relative location to the referent. The people or things being referred to must be explicitly stated and located in space before they can be referred to. For example, if the signer wants to discuss the interaction between two people, or between people and things, each person or thing must be identified and located in space first. Then the signer can index them or refer to them by simply pointing. If they change relative locations, then the signer must make it clear how the people and objects have moved to new locations. For example if a person is referred to in the right of the signing space and the house is referred to in the left of the signing space, later, the signer can reassign the spaces to two people or two houses. When this happens the signer has *reconstructed space*. (see Taylor 2002 p.74)

Several common errors consistently occur within spatial referencing. According to Taylor, the first occurs when the interpreter does not correctly understand to whom the signer is addressing a question or comment. For example, when the signer is speaking to an audience, an interpreter might possibly misunderstand what the speaker intended and interpret the question as if it were directed to the interpreter rather than the audience.

Another common error within spatial referencing is misidentifying the recipient of the action. When the signer has established people, objects, or concepts in a certain location, the signer may also "restructure space" or use the space assigned to the person, object, or concept to describe characteristics, features, and other information about that referent. Sometimes this restructuring of space is misunderstood and misinterpreted. It is also possible that the signer can combine characterization with restructuring space. Taylor's (2002) example indicates that the signer can change perspective and "take on the character" of the recipient of the action. An accurate interpretation will indicate where the participants were in relation to each other and where and how the action of one impacted the other.

Within the category of errors related to space we also find errors related to "distant cohesion." Taylor (2002) explains that the signer can establish a referent in space and that space is "held" for that referent. The signer can "come back" to this point at a later time. The interpreter must remember which referent occupies which location, even if the referent is not referred to again for some period of time.

Sometimes the signer's nondominant hand can be used to express spatial relationships. Taylor's (2002) research indicates that meaning and importance of the switch to the nondominant hand is often misinterpreted. In ASL, space is also used to show a change in perspective such as arriving at a building, approaching the building, and entering it. In each of these instances, the interpreter must correctly understand and interpret how the perspective has shifted. Taylor says, "The interpreter must follow the signing journey" (p. 78).

Another category of possible errors uncovered in Taylor's (2002) research relates to the importance of *utterance boundaries*. Just as sentences in English have beginnings and endings, so do sentences in ASL. According to Nicodemus, (2009) "Boundaries are especially crucial in the larger picture of communication because individuals rely on these points to segment a language stream into constituents, such as topics, phrases, and sentences that make discourse more comprehensible" (p. 1). Nicodemus also says, "In spoken languages, boundary points may be characterized by modulations in rhythm, stress, loudness, intonation, pausing, and duration. In signed languages, both manual and non-manual movements are used to segment a stream of discourse. These patterns, referred to as prosody, give important cues to the syntactic structure of sentences, as well as to which parts of the sentence are in prominence" (p.1). ASL has specific types of discourse markers that interpreters must understand and interpret correctly. Misunderstanding a lexical item intended as a sentence boundary can lead to a misinterpretation. Taylor's example uses the sign UNDERSTAND+++ as a sentence boundary, in the same way that BUT can be used as a sentence boundary. However, when UNDER-

STAND+++ is misunderstood, it is interpreted as "Do you understand?" Other utterance boundaries that are misunderstood and thus misinterpreted include pausing, eye blinks or head nods, shift in body stance, lowering the hands, and introducing a new topic. Eye blinks and head nods can serve as "punctuation" to show the end of the utterance. A shift in stance can be used to shift from the present to the future or to change characterization. When the signer's hands are lowered, it indicates a pause or change of subject. Taylor explains that when interpreters fail to convey an utterance boundary, the resulting message can be inaccurate because the information from one segment of discourse is construed to be part of the next segment of discourse instead of as separate topics.

The next major category of errors studied in Taylor's (2002) research is *handedness of the signer.* Her data suggest that errors in ASL to English interpreting occur more frequently when information is conveyed with the left hand or when handedness is switched during discourse. According to Hardyck and Petrinovich (1977), approximately 8 to 15% of the general adult population is left handed. If we generalize this statistic to the deaf population, we can infer that most signers are right handed. This means that interpreters are more likely to have experience reading right-handed signers than left-handed signers and, as a result, be more likely to make mistakes when interpreting for left-handed signers. Sometimes signers switch from signing with their right (or left) hand to signing some parts of the utterance with their other hand. Whether the signer is left handed or switches hands, information that appears on the nondominant hand may be omitted. According to Taylor, the nondominant hand may also be used for other important discourse markers, such as structuring space or creating emphasis. Because interpreters have less experience with seeing these types of constructions, there is a greater likelihood of interpreting errors when the nondominant hand conveys these types of information.

The exercises that follow emphasize comprehension at the discourse level, one aspect of cognitive processing. Specifically, the ASL features discussed in Unit 2 will be highlighted in the exercises, along with a continuing emphasis on fingerspelled word recognition.

EXERCISES IN COMPREHENSION OF ASL DISCOURSE

EXERCISE 2.1

Summer on the Farm

BEN BAHAN

Directions

This exercise has two selections. The first short segment allows you to get to know the signer and become accustomed to his signing style and the second segment allows you to focus on comprehension of his message.

The second selection is approximately 3 minutes long. Watch the entire selection once and then answer the study questions in ASL as best as you can. Watch the selection as many times as you need to fully understand the selection, using slow motion if needed, and answer any remaining study questions.

Get to Know the Signer

This short segment allows you to get acquainted with the signer. Watch the selection and replay it until you can answer the following questions in complete sentences using ASL. You do not need to record your responses.

1. Where does he currently work and how long has he been there?

    _____

2. Where did he work prior to his current position and how long was he there?

    _____

3. Which discipline does he teach?

    _____

4. Where did he grow up, what school did he attend as a child, and where did he go to college?

    _____

5. What are the names of his wife and children?

_____

_____

Study Questions

1. Correct recognition of all fingerspelled words is necessary for complete ASL comprehension. Below, you will find a list of English words that represent the translations of fingerspelled words from this selection. Each word will play at regular speed, in slow motion, and again at regular speed. If a fingerspelled word appeared several times in the selection, it will only appear once here. Play the selected fingerspelled words five times until you are sure you can easily recognize each word.

   After you have studied and can easily recognize each fingerspelled word, turn on your video recording device and spell each fingerspelled word clearly, using it in a sentence. Do not rush through the spelling. Compare your spelling with that of the signer. Note any differences in your productive fingerspelling compared with that of the signer. Practice spelling each word several more times, working to match the signer's spelling.

   ### English Translations of Fingerspelled Words:
   Metro, New York City
   South Dakota
   Ranch
   Back (lexicalized)
   Pickup truck
   City
   Hill
   Corral

2. Review the selection again and look for examples of facial grammar that indicates yes–no or topicalization. Write the time codes in the space provided. You may want to play the selection in slow motion to assist you in finding these features. Examples of the facial grammar features are shown in clips on your DVD.

Example of topicalization

01:15:17;24 to 01:15:18;19

Example of yes–no question

01:15:21;18 to 01:15:22;28

_____

_____

_____

3. Review the selection again, focusing on ASL referencing and spatial relationships. Answer the following questions in ASL. There are many more examples of referencing and spatial relationships in the selection.

   a. Ben refers to something with his index finger two times from 01:14:20;18 to 01:14:25;22. What is Ben referencing with his index finger?

   b. What are the brothers checking on the ranch?

   c. What are they looking at on the cow?

   d. What is the mother cow tied to?

   e. Where is the calf in relation to its mother?

Identify five additional examples and write the time codes.

_____

_____

_____

_____

_____

4. Watch the entire selection, looking for examples of distant cohesion and write the time codes in the space provided. You will find pairs of time codes. The first time code will show where something was established by the signer. The second time code will show where the signer referred back to what was established. Some suggestions are provided to help you get started.

   a. What is Ben referring to over his right shoulder at 01:15:10;07 to 01:15:12;01 and 01:16:06;11 to 01:16:08;17?

   b. Note where the mother cow is first located and how Ben remains consistent in referring to the cow.

   c. Note how when Ben is riding his horse, following the others, he consistently uses the space ahead of him to refer to the open range where the mother and baby cow are and how he uses the space behind him to represent the ranch.

_____

_____

_____

_____

5. Watch the selection in slow motion and look for utterance boundaries in the selection. Remember to look for hands moving to neutral space, eye blink, head tilting back, or some combination of these. Write the beginnig time codes for each boundary that you find. Examples are shown on the DVD.

Examples of utterance boundaries

01:14:17;19

01:14:38;18

01:15:06;05

01:15:13;05

_____

_____

_____

_____

_____

6. Watch the selection again. Has your comprehension improved?

EXERCISE 2.2

Family Vacation

JESSICA OLSEN-DUNBAR

Directions

This exercise has two selections. The first short segment allows you to get to know the signer and become accustomed to her signing style and the second segment allows you to focus on comprehension of her message.

The second selection is approximately 2 minutes long. Watch the entire selection once and then answer the study questions in ASL as best as you can. Watch the selection as many times as you need to fully understand the selection, using slow motion if needed, and answer any remaining study questions.

Get to Know the Signer

This short segment allows you to get acquainted with the signer. Watch the selection and replay it until you can answer the following questions in complete sentences using ASL. You do not need to record your responses.

1. Where is she from?

_____

2. What kind of school did she go to?

_____

3. Who in her family is deaf?

_____

4. What sports did she play in high school?

   _____

5. What did she major in at college?

   _____

6. Where does she work now and how long has she been there?

   _____

Study Questions

1. Correct recognition of all fingerspelled words is necessary for complete ASL comprehension. Below you will find a list of English words that represent the translations of fingerspelled words from this selection. Each word will play at regular speed, in slow motion, and again at regular speed. If a fingerspelled word appeared several times in the selection, it will only appear once here. Play the selected fingerspelled words five times until you are sure you can easily recognize each word.

   After you have studied and can easily recognize each fingerspelled word, turn on your video recording device and spell each fingerspelled word clearly, using it in a sentence. Do not rush through the spelling. Compare your spelling with that of the signer. Note any differences in your productive fingerspelling compared with that of the signer. Practice spelling each word several more times, working to match the signer's spelling.

   ### English Translations of Fingerspelled Words:

   Orlando Florida (FLA)
   Walt Disney World (WD)
   Epcot
   Sea World
   Sea gulls
   Surf
   Ocean
   Sand
   Castles
   Back (lexicalized)
   Hotel
   Rent
   Minutes (min)
   Exit

2. Review the selection again and look for examples of facial grammar that indicates yes–no, topicalization, or wh questions. Write the time codes in the space provided. You may want to play the selection in slow motion to assist you in finding these features. Examples are shown on the DVD.

Example of yes–no question

01:19:38;00 to 01:19:39;10

Example of topicalization

01:18:54;26 to 01:18:59;02

Example of wh question

01:19:47;14 to 01:19:49;28

_____

_____

_____

3. Review the selection again, focusing on ASL referencing and spatial relationships. Record yourself answering the following questions in ASL.

    a. What is Jessica pointing to at 01:18:40;14?

    b. What is Jessica feeding?

    c. Who is the driver of the rental car and who is seated behind the driver? Who is next to the driver and where are her brothers seated?

    d. Where was this car in relation to Jessica's family car?

    e. Who noticed the people signing in the next car?

    f. Which classifier represents the car Jessica is in?

4. Watch the selection in slow motion and note the utterance boundaries in the selection. Remember to look for hands moving to neutral space, eye blink, head tilting back, or some combination of these. Examples are provided to help you get started in identifying sentence boundaries. Find five more and write the time codes in the space provided below.

    Examples of utterance boundaries

01:18:42;20

01:19:15;10

01:19:21;02

01:19:35;01

_____

_____

_____

_____

5. Look for examples of distant cohesion and write the time codes in the space provided. Examples:

    a. Jessica maintains the location of Orlando to her right.

    b. Jessica maintains the location of the seagulls as she refers back to them to feed them.

    c. The location of the two cars (referents) remains constant in this segment.

    _____

    _____

    _____

_____

_____

6. Watch the selection again. Has your comprehension improved?

EXERCISE 2.3

My Garden

MISSY KEAST

Directions

This exercise has two selections. The first short segment allows you to get to know the signer and become accustomed to her signing style and the second segment allows you to focus on comprehension of her message.

The second selection is approximately 6 minutes long. Watch the entire selection once and then answer the study questions in ASL to the best of your ability. Watch the selection as many times as you need to fully understand the selection, using slow motion if needed, and answer any remaining study questions in ASL using complete sentences. Be sure to record your responses.

Get to Know the Signer

This short segment allows you to get acquainted with the signer. Watch the selection and replay it until you can answer the following questions in ASL using complete sentences.

1. Why does she prefer her older name sign?

    _____

2. How many siblings does she have? How many are deaf? How many people in her family sign?

    _____

3. How old is her daughter?

    _____

Study Questions

1. Correct recognition of all fingerspelled words is necessary for complete ASL comprehension. Below, you will find a list of English words that represent the translations of fingerspelled words. Play each fingerspelled word five times until you are sure you can easily recognize the word. Use slow motion to help you study the fingerspelled words.

    The fingerspelled words appear in the selection and in the clips for the study questions. The clips on the DVD are numbered to correspond with the numbers of the study questions in your book. If a fingerspelled word appears more than once in the selection, it is only listed here once. Study each fingerspelled word until you feel confident that you comprehend it at slow and regular speed. Turn on your recording device and spell each fingerspelled word in this selection as clearly and carefully as you can. Do not rush through the spelling. Compare your productive fingerspelling with that of the signer. Practice spelling the word several more times, working to make it look more like the signer's.

    English Translations of Fingerspelled Words:

    Backyard

    Soil

    Rich

    Dust

    Bush

    Fig

    Lemon

    Citrus

    Grapefruit

    Bamboo

    Irrigation

    Canal

    Pipe

    Lake

    Garden

    Off

    Dirt

    Truck

    Then

    Seeds

    Spinach

    Pepper

Squash

Space

Scarecrow

Dog

Own

Organic

Reality

Back (lexicalized)

Plastic

Then

Net

2. Review the selection again and look for examples of facial grammar that indicates yes–no, topicalization, or wh questions. Write the time codes in the space provided. Play the selection in slow motion to assist you in finding these features. Examples are shown on the DVD.

Examples of topicalization

01:22:14;14 to 01:22:18;10

01:22:38;03 to 01:22:39;15

Example of wh question

01:25:06;25 to 01:25:08;22

_____

_____

_____

_____

3. Review the entire selection again, focusing on ASL referencing and spatial relationships. Record yourself answering the following questions in ASL.

a. What is Missy referring to here?

01:22:17;10

b. What is Missy referring to here?

01:23:03;18

c. Missy's torso and gaze are turned to her left. What is she looking at?

01:23:10;00

d. What is Missy pointing to?

01:23:10;20

e. What is Missy looking at?

01:23:37;28

f. Who or what is Missy looking at? Who is she talking to?

01:23:48;18

g. Who is talking?

01:23:50;14

h. What does the truck back up to? Where does it dump the dirt?

01:24:27;00

i. At 01:27:16;00 Missy turns her torso and gaze to the right. What is the significance of this? To whom is she speaking?

01:27:16;00

j. At 01:27:17;11 Missy turns her torso and gaze to her left. What is the significance of this? Who is making this comment to whom?

01:27:17;11

k. Starting at 01:27:17;22 who is the other person and what did that person say to Missy?

l. What is Missy holding in her left hand?

01:28:02;26

m. What does her right hand represent here?

01:28:03;26

4. Watch the selection in slow motion to develop your acuity in detecting utterance boundaries. Look for hands moving to neutral space, eye blink, followed by head tilting back, or all three. Hint: This signer also holds the last sign of an utterance. Find at least five more examples and write the beginning time codes in the space provided.

Examples of utterance boundaries

01:22:10;03 to 01:22:14;14

01:24:00;24

_____

_____

_____

_____

5. Look for examples of distant cohesion and write the time codes in the space provided.

_____

_____

_____

6. Watch the selection again. Has your comprehension improved?

Progress Tracking Sheet

This sheet is designed to help you keep track of which exercises you have completed and how well you have done on these exercises. A rating system is presented for you to rate the outcomes of your work on the exercises. After completing each exercise, fill in the tracking sheet. Rate your performance on the exercises using this scale: excellent (no serious errors) = 5 points; good (some errors, but not serious) = 4 points; fair (many errors, some serious) = 3 points; not satisfactory (many errors, most are serious) = 2 points; poor (missed the point of the exercise—must redo) =1 point

Exercise Number and Name	Date	First Performance Rating	Second Performance Rating	Questions and Reminders
Exercise 2.1 Summer on the Farm				
Exercise 2.2 Family Vacation				
Exercise 2.3 My Garden				

UNIT

3

Memory

Unit 1 focues on comprehension and Unit 2 brought your attention to deeper levels of comprehension. Unit 3 brings us to the topic of memory and its relationship to the interpreting process. Memory is the retention of information over time. It is also a mental activity for recalling information that has been learned or experienced. Memory involves receiving, retaining, and retrieving data that are important for our everyday living and even more important in the interpreting process. Gile's (1995) Effort Model of simultaneous interpreting identifies memory as one of the three main efforts in interpreting. Interpreting relies on additional aspects of memory such as short-term, intermediate, long-term, kinetic, episodic, procedural, visual, and auditory memory. First we look at some basic terms and information about memory and then we apply this information to the interpreting process.

When information reaches a person, it first must be *encoded*. Encoding allows incoming information to be "coded" appropriately for storage through one or more modalities or mechanisms. The three main modalities are *visual, acoustic,* and *semantic*. Visual information enters memory as "pictures" or mental images, rather than sounds. Acoustic coding allows auditory information to be rehearsed using an "inner voice" or subvocal sounds. Semantic encoding is achieved through obtaining information, such as from reading a book or listening to a lecture (Baddeley, 1990).

Once information has been encoded, it is subject to at least two main types of memory processes: short-term or long-term. *Short-term memory* (STM), or working memory, refers to the amount or bits of information you can hold in your head at any given time and lasts for a few seconds or up to a minute, depending on how important the information is to you. This is the type of memory you use to remember phone numbers, the name of someone you just met, and zip codes. A key feature of STM is *attention,* followed by *registration.* This type of memory focuses on whatever you are concentrating on or paying attention to at the moment. For something to enter your short-term memory, you must pay attention to it for a quarter of a second (Sperling, 1960; Crowden, 1982). This fact shows us why it is important for interpreters to learn to focus attention while interpreting.

> *Registration* allows the brain to notice new information. The cerebral cortex registers messages from our eyes, ears, and touch sensors via specific nerve pathways. This stimulus is held for a fraction of a second in the "sensory memory." But unless you pay attention to the image for approximately eight uninterrupted seconds to encode it into short-term memory, it will be lost. The slightest interference at this stage will wipe the newly acquired information from our consciousness. (http://www.audiblox2000.com/learning_disabilities/memory.htm)

Because the information in STM is not rehearsed or entered into long-term memory, it is remembered only for a short time and then it "decays" or is forgotten. The duration of STM is very short, probably about 30 seconds (Atkinson & Shiffrin, 1968; Hebb, 1949), but researchers do not agree on the exact duration. Peterson (1959) reported it to be 6–12 seconds.

Long-term memory results from a deliberate attempt to remember or use the information, which creates neural pathways that allow you to recall the information later. Long-term memory can last a minute, days, weeks, or even years. Long-term memories can be conscious or unconscious and can be viewed as the "repository" of all our knowledge. Long-term memory allows you to recall general information learned previously, past experiences, or rules and has three types: episodic, semantic, and procedural.

Schweda-Nicholson points out that long-term memory has two broad categories, procedural memory and propositional memory. Procedural memory is used to perform actions such as typing or rollerblading after they have been learned. It is no longer necessary to think of each step in the process. Using your muscles to do something such as play a sport, play an instrument, or drive a car creates *procedural memory.* This type of memory requires physical action to learn the skill. Procedural memory is linked to motor memory. One of the key factors in being able to analyze the incoming message during the interpreting process is memory. It is vital that you remember the incoming message long enough to analyze it.

Propositional memory is the memory that allows a person to remember concepts. Propositional memory can be further subdivided into episodic and semantic memory.

Episodic memory results primarily from experiences and events and relies on sensory input such as sound, sight, smell, and touch. Many times, episodic memories are linked to the emotion you experienced at the time the memory was made, such as the smell of your favorite food being cooked for you when you were a child. According to Tulvig (1983), episodic memory, allows people to remember events from their own lifetimes.

Semantic memory allows you to remember specific information, like facts you learn from books. Tulvig (1983) says semantic memory is general knowledge that is retained, regardless of how it was learned. For example, you may be able to answer the question; "In what city is the Eiffel Tower located?" without knowing exactly where you learned this fact. Semantic memory is an accumulation of experiences and facts over time.

Retrieval allows you to "find" information that you have stored. It relies on a process similar to finding a folder or file in your computer. If you have tried to remember something and it seemed like it was just on the tip of your tongue but you could not recall it, that is an example of difficulties in retrieval (*http://www.audiblox2000.com/learning_disabilities/memory.htm*).

Forgetting occurs for several different reasons. When storage capacity is at its maximum limit, existing information is *displaced* with newer information and the older information is no longer available (Waugh & Norman, 1965). Over time, if information is not used, it tends to *decay* (Baddeley et al., 1975). *Interference* occurs when there are two types of information in memory and one distorts the other (Keppel & Underwood, 1962). In the next section, you will see how the basic memory processes are related to the complex process of interpreting.

The Role of Memory in the Interpreting Process

Interpreters must be able to accurately remember the content of the source message long enough to analyze, comprehend, transfer, and reformulate it into the target language. Schweda Nicholson (1996) points out the relevance of procedural memory to interpreting. This is the kind of memory that is evoked without conscious awareness. Schweda Nicholson posited,

> It has been suggested that much of the process of interpretation (especially simultaneous) becomes almost automatic with practice. In other words, the procedural knowledge necessary for accomplishing the task of [simultaneous interpretation] is activated independently and unconsciously, thereby leaving the bulk of attentional resources available for semantic analysis of incoming source language material as well as formulation output and monitoring of the target language rendition (p. 102).

This means that although the process of simultaneous interpreting is very complex and demanding, some aspects of it can become less effortful (not effortless). Two aspects that will almost always require high levels of effort are determining what is meant by the incoming message and formulating the outgoing message. One of the key factors in being able to analyze the incoming message is memory. It is vital that you remember the incoming message long enough for it to be analyzed.

Interpreters are generally not responsible for remembering the content of messages that they have interpreted after they are finished interpreting. However, memory is an important part of the interpreting process. The various components of working memory and long-term memory are important for interpreters. Experienced interpreters tend to shift quickly and efficiently between working memory and long-term memory stores without conscious realization. Schweda Nicholson (1996) emphasizes that there is a constant interplay between working and long-term memory during the interpreting process. It is as if interpreters can quickly access what they know about a topic and tap into that knowledge to help them process the incoming message.

General world knowledge falls into the category of long-term memory. Gile (1995) refers to this kind of knowledge as ELK. The more you know or remember about a topic, the better when it comes to interpreting. This is part of why it is easier to interpret a speech when the topic is familiar. Because ELK is so valuable for interpreters, they often feel it is very important to read daily newspapers and be as well educated as possible.

If memory skills are well developed, there is a much higher chance that the resulting interpreting will be accurate. Certainly, practice in specific skills can cause those skills to become more automatic.

Gile (1995) suggests that interpreting requires a certain amount of "mental energy" and that the requirements of the interpreting task must not exceed the interpreter's available supply of mental energy. When the demands of the job exceed the interpreter's mental energy, the interpreting performance will suffer. This idea of limited supplies of mental energy adds support to the notion that it is worthwhile to reduce the amount of effort associated with specific parts of the interpreting process. Often, this effort can be reduced by practice on the component parts of the interpretation process so that the components become more nearly automatic.

This brief overview of some of the theoretical aspects of memory and memory as it relates to interpreting forms a foundation for the practical, skills-based exercises that follow.

Additional Reading

For further reading and suggestions about improving memory skills see the following works.

Baddeley, A. (1976). *The psychology of memory*. New York: Basic Books.

Herrmann, D. J. (1990). *Super memory*. Emmaus, PA: Rodale.

Gordon, B. (1995). *Memory*. New York: Master Media.

Higbee, K. L. (1988). *Your memory* (2nd ed.). Englewood Cliffs, NJ: Prentice Hall.

Lorayne, H., & Lucas, J. (1974). *The memory book*. New York: Stein & Day.

West, R. (1985). *Memory fitness over forty*. Gainesville, FL: Triad. (This is a fact sheet from the Administration on Aging and the National Institute on Neurological Disorders and Stroke)

Sharma, V. P. http://www.mindpub.com/art079.htm

http://www.helpguide.org/life/improving_memory.htm

http://www.thememorypage.net/tut.htm

http://frank.mtsu.edu/~studskl/mem.html

MEMORY EXERCISES

EXERCISE 3.1

Vegetarian Viewpoint

BROOKE BUDZINSKI

Directions

This exercise has two selections. The first short segment allows you to get to know the signer and become accustomed to her signing style and the second segment allows you to focus on practicing memory skills.

The second selection is approximately 2 minutes long. Find this selection on your DVD. Be sure you can see the screen clearly. After watching this selection once, answer Study Question 1 in ASL. Watch the DVD again and look for details that you may have missed. Answer the rest of the study questions in ASL, using complete sentences. For example you would sign the ASL equivalent of "Many Americans are overweight because . . . " You may find it helpful to watch the selection in slow motion.

Get to Know the Signer

This short segment allows you to get acquainted with the signer. Watch the selection and replay it until you can answer the following questions. Respond in ASL. You do not need to record your responses.

1. Where did she grow up?

_____

2. When did she enter Gallaudet University?

_____

3. What happened after she graduated?

_____

4. What does Brooke do now?

_____

Study Questions

1. In ASL, recount as many details you can remember about this selection. Record your answers.

2. According to Brooke, why are so many Americans overweight?

3. What historical time period does she refer to in describing how people ate in earlier times? Respond in ASL using a complete sentence. Record your answer.

4. What did people have to do to make cookies during the time period she refers to? Respond in ASL using a complete sentence. Record your answer.

5. How did the cookies taste when they were ready to eat?

6. How did eating cookies affect their diet and weight?

7. What does she suggest that Americans do to improve their diet?

8. Why does she support vegetarianism?

9. What types of meat do true vegetarians eat?

10. Explain in ASL what the following signs mean.

01:29:07;21

01:29:22;03

01:29:25;08

11. What strategies did you use to focus your attention on the speaker's message? What strategies did you use to remember the message?

_____

_____

EXERCISE 3.2

The Last Yellow Rose

TROY KOTSUR

Directions

This exercise has two selections. The first short segment allows you to get to know the signer and become accustomed to his signing style and the second segment allows you to focus on memory skills.

The second selection is approximately 4 minutes long. Find this selection on your DVD. Be sure you can see the screen clearly. After watching this selection once, answer Study Question 1 in ASL. Watch the DVD again and look for details that you may have missed. Answer the remaining study questions in ASL, using complete sentences. Record your answers. You may find it helpful to watch the selection in slow motion.

Get to Know the Signer

This short segment allows you to get acquainted with the signer and is about 2 minutes long. Watch the selection and replay it until you can answer the following questions. Respond in ASL using the spaces below for written answers. You do not need to record your responses.

1. What is his middle name?

    _____

2. Where was he born?

    _____

3. How many siblings does he have and are they deaf?

    _____

4. Where did he attend school and how long was he there?

    _____

5. Where else did he attend school and what sports did he play?

    _____

6. How many other deaf students were on the teams?

    _____

7. Where did he go after high school graduation and how long did he stay there?

    _____

8. What did he do next? Name the group he joined.

    _____

9. Where did he travel with the National Theater of the Deaf?

_____

10. Where does he live now? Which theatre company is he with now?

11. What are his activities now?

_____

12. What does he hope for the future?

_____

Study Questions

1. In ASL, recount as many details you can remember about this selection. Record your answer.

2. Is this a true story? Who is it about?

3. What is the title of the story?

4. What did he discover when he came into the house?

5. What did he decide to do to make her feel better?

6. What did he purchase before he began telling the story and where did he put it?

7. Where did the main character in the story look to find a yellow rose?

8. Where is the last yellow rose in the world located?

9. Why is it important that the rose be yellow?

10. What did he do when he arrived in South Africa?

11. What happened to the 20th person as they walked through the jungle?

12. What happened to the next 4 people who were killed?

13. What happened to the next person who was killed?

14. What did he do when he finally saw the yellow rose?

15. In the end, how many people were left and who was it?

16. How does the story end?

EXERCISE 3.3

I Learned Something

C. J. JONES

Directions

This exercise has two selections. The first short segment allows you to get to know the signer and become accustomed to his signing style and the second segment allows you to focus on memory skills.

The second selection is approximately 5 minutes long. Find this selection on your DVD. Be sure you can see the screen clearly. After watching this selection once, answer Study Question 1 in ASL. Watch the DVD again and look for details that you may have missed. Answer the remaining study questions in ASL, using complete sentences. Record your answer. You may find it helpful to watch the selection in slow motion.

Get to Know the Signer

This short segment allows you to get acquainted with the signer and is about 2 minutes long. Watch the selection and replay it until you can answer the following questions. Respond in ASL. You do not need to record your responses.

1. Where is he from?

_____

2. Are his parents and siblings deaf or hearing?

_____

3. At what age did C. J. lose his hearing and what was the cause?

_____

_____

4. What was his parent's reaction to his deafness?

_____

_____

5. Where did he go to school?

_____

6. What was his work after college?

_____

7. What famous Broadway show was he in?

_____

8. What does he do now?

_____

_____

Study Questions

1. In ASL, recount as many details you can remember about this selection. Record your answer.

2. What did he look like when he went to the school for the deaf?

3. What does this sign mean in this context?

01:39:57;27

4. What does this sign mean in this context?

01:39:59;16

5. What does this sign mean in this context?

01:40:07;17

6. Who is this dialogue between?

7. What does this sign mean in this context?

01:40:23;09

8. What did his dad want him to become?

9. Who is he referring to here?

01:40:36;16

10. How did his friends encourage him?

11. How did he look to the coach?

12. What did the coach make him do?

13. Did he do the push-ups correctly?

14. How did he think he performed during the tryouts?

15. What was his reaction to being selected?

16. What does this sign mean in this context?

01:41:28;09

17. What does this sign mean in this context?

01:41:33;16

18. What do these signs mean in this context?

01:41:36;14

19. What do these signs mean in this context?

01:41:55;12

20. What does this sign mean in this context?

01:42:02;03

21. What do these signs mean in this context?

01:42:04;06

22. What did the coach tell him to do?

Progress Tracking Sheet

This sheet is designed to help you keep track of which exercises you have completed and how well you have done on these exercises. A rating system is presented for you to rate the outcomes of your work on the exercises. After completing each exercise and activity, fill in the tracking sheet. Your instructor may ask you to copy and submit the tracking sheet for each unit. Rate your performance on the exercises using the following scale: excellent (no serious errors) = 5 points; good (some errors, but not serious) = 4 points; fair (many errors, some serious) = 3 points; not satisfactory (many errors, most are serious) = 2 points; poor (missed the point of the exercise—must redo) =1 point.

Exercise Number and Name	Date	First Performance Rating	Second Performance Rating	Questions and Reminders
Exercise 3.1 Vegetarian Viewpoint				
Exercise 3.2 The Last Yellow Rose				
Exercise 3.3 I Learned Something				

UNIT 4

Immediate Repetition

Repetition means to perform again. Immediate repetition means to perform again without delay. This type of repetition starts as soon as the viewer has seen enough of the signed message to begin repeating it. Immediate repetition uncovers the ability to find the minimal length of time behind the signer and maintain that distance. The distance in time that separates the signer's utterance and the repetition of that utterance by the interpreter is a subject of much interest in interpreting. This distance is called lag time, processing time, or decalage. All of these terms refer to how much time has elapsed between when the speaker says something and when the interpreter renders the interpretation of that same utterance. By practicing the skill of immediate repetition and, later, delayed repetition, interpreters can get the feel for what it is like to maintain enough cognitive control over their repetitions to stay immediately behind the speaker or a phrase behind the speaker. Later, during actual simultaneous interpreting, the ability to control the amount of processing time becomes a valuable asset for interpreters.

The ability to perform immediate repetition includes self-monitoring. In this context, self-monitoring includes being aware of what you are signing and comparing that with the original message. Lambert (1989) calls immediate repetition phonemic shadowing and describes it as listening and speaking at the same time when what is spoken is the same as what is listened to. She says it is a "paced auditory task, which involves the immediate vocalization of auditory stimuli, i.e., a word-for-word repetition in the same language, parrot-style of a message presented through headphones." This kind of repetition means that each syllable is repeated as soon as it is heard. All of these points can be applied to a signed as well as an auditory message. Whether the message is auditory or visual, the process of immediate repetition tends to rely primarily on working memory. Because of the limits of working memory, people usually cannot remember the messages used to practice immediate repetition because there is not enough time to process the message into meaningful units. Remember that immediate repetition is a practice that helps build control over processing time, but does not encourage deeper levels of analysis and comprehension. During simultaneous interpreting both skills are needed but are separated here to allow you to develop better control of the process.

The Role of Immediate Repetition in the Interpreting Process

Immediate repetition in one's first language is used routinely prior to admission into an interpreter education program as a screening technique to determine whether the prospective interpreter can listen and speak (or watch signs and sign simultaneously). It is equally important to be able to perform immediate repletion in your second language. Knowing that you can watch and repeat ASL will help build your cognitive abilities and self-confidence.

DeGroot's (1997) analysis of recent research suggests that the skill of immediate repetition shares many components with simultaneous interpreting. DeGroot points out that the processes of immediate repetition and simultaneous interpreting both require comprehending and producing speech simultaneously.

There are at least seven reasons why immediate repetition is a valuable and interesting tool for interpreters. Here are some of the things that the ability to use immediate repetition can tell us. De Groot's seven reasons are expanded below.

1. *The interpreter is not distracted by his or her own signing during the process.* When you watch ASL and practice repeating exactly what you saw, it requires great focus and concentration not to be distracted by your own signing. When you can watch and sign at the same time without being distracted by your own signing it indicates high levels of concentration. Concentration and the ability to remain focused are both essential to the interpreting process.

2. *There is an ability to manage this aspect of simultaneity.* If the interpreter has the ability to watch ASL and immediately repeat, it means that a sophisticated level of managing one of the complex tasks within the interpreting process. Immediate repletion in your second language may be more difficult than in your first language. Being able to watch and repeat indicates that the ability to handle more complex, interlingual skills related to simultaneous interpreting.

3. *There is an ability to simultaneously perform a synthesis and segmentation of discourse elements.* This means that the interpreter can grasp the larger meaning of the message while still being able to break the

message down into smaller parts for processing. When watching an ASL message you are consciously or unconsciously extracting the meaning or ideas from a series of signs, rather than remembering individual signs. As interpreters we attempt to remember ideas and how the ideas are grouped. When we remember an idea we have remembered a *segment* of the information. We use the process of segmentation in immediate repetition and in simultaneous interpreting. Because segmentation is an important underlying skill, it is best to practice it separately before beginning simultaneous interpreting. After you have segmented the incoming information, in order to reproduce it in either the same language or in a different language, you use a process called synthesis to recreate the message. If repeating, you use the exact words or signs you heard in the source. If you are interpreting you synthesize the message in the target language.

4. *There is an ability to reformulate the text* (Kurz, 1992). This means that the interpreter is able to listen and to create the text again. Reformulation during repetition is made possible by fully comprehending the incoming message and having adequate language skill to reproduce the message in exactly the same terms. Reformulation in simultaneous interpreting is a more complex skill that builds on intralingual reformulation. During simultaneous interpreting the interpreter reformulates the message into the target language.

5. *There may be an ability to monitor accuracy of output.* With practice, the ability to check for accuracy usually improves. Interpreters need to be able to check their own interpreting in real time. This is an extremely complex and difficult skill. Because the ability to check one's own work in simultaneous interpreting is so difficult, it is best to begin to gain control of the process of checking one's own output by practicing repetition within a language.

6. *There may be an ability to monitor distance behind the source.* We know that interpreters who have good control over their processing time tend to make fewer errors. Gaining control of processing time is a specific skill that is best practiced through immediate repetition drills and exercises. If you have developed the ability to consciously monitor your processing time relative to the speed of the incoming message, then you have developed one of the key resources you will need for successful simultaneous interpreting.

7. *Interference can be attended to or filtered out.* In the real world of interpreting, interpreters must work within a context that includes visual and auditory noise that can be distracting and disruptive. Despite various forms of interference, it is necessary to be able to filter out the aspects of the environment that do not relate to the interpreting process. At first you may find that noise or visual disturbances prevent you from doing your best work. But with practice you can develop

greater resistance to non-essential information in your environment and gain better control over your concentration for either repletion or simultaneous interpreting.

Gaining control of attention and the other specific aspects of the cognitive processes in the interpreting process are vital to your success as an interpreter. There are real-world professional uses for immediate repetition. For example, when two interpreters work together as a team, one serves as the backup interpreter. The backup interpreter can sometimes provide missing words or sentences to the interpreter who is speaking if the working interpreter has missed part of the message. In this case, the working interpreter listens to the backup interpreter and simply repeats the information provided by the backup interpreter. Then the working interpreter goes on with the interpreting process. The information from the backup interpreter may seem like interference. Interference here refers to any additional distraction occurs during the interpreting process. For the interpretation to continue, the information provided by the backup interpreter must be attended to quickly and accurately, rather than filtered out or ignored. In the case of ASL to English interpreting, this requires the intake of ongoing visual information from the signer and incoming and possibly unexpected auditory information from the backup interpreter.

Being able to speak while listening, or watch signing and sign, is an essential skill in the interpreting process. Lambert (1989) indicates four categories into which these performances tend to fall: (1) people who find listening and speaking at the same time effortless, (2) people who can repeat the beginning of a sentence but can't complete the repetition properly, (3) people who use the pauses in the text as a time for the repetition, and (4) people who are totally incoherent but keep talking. Ideally, with practice, immediate repetition can become effortless. When immediate repetition becomes effortless, then one more aspect of simultaneity is controlled by the interpreter's cognitive processing ability. When a cognitive process such as this one becomes more effortless, more of the interpreter's cognitive processing can be devoted to other aspects of the interpreting process.

EXERCISES IN IMMEDIATE REPETITION

EXERCISE 4.1

Autobiography

ANNE MARIE BAER

Directions

The selection is approximately 2 minutes long. It is important to be sure you understand the passage before practicing repeating. Take time to study and understand the passage first. Answer the comprehension questions in ASL. Recording your answers to the comprehension questions is optional. Complete the repetition and answer the study questions. You will need a quiet place to work where you will not be interrupted and where you can record your repetition and responses. Record yourself while you are engaged in immediate repetition. Begin repeating as soon as the selection on the DVD starts. After you finish your repetition, review your work and record your answers to the study questions in ASL. Remember, during this exercise you are not required to remember what you repeat. Be sure to study the passage first.

Comprehension Questions

1. Where was she born?

2. Where did her parents meet?

3. Where is her mother from?

4. What year did her parents marry?

5. How many siblings does Anne Marie have?

6. What is she studying now?

Study Questions

1. Was your signing intelligible?

2. Did your own signing distract you or prevent you from attending to the signer? What strategy can you develop to overcome this distraction?

3. Did watching the signer interfere with your ability to repeat? What strategy can you develop to overcome this distraction?

4. Repeat the exercise and see whether your ASL is more understandable the second time. Does the syntax of your repetition better match the speaker's?

In a second trial, the work should be much improved.

EXERCISE 4.2

My Involvement in Black Deaf Student Union
AYUK OGORK

Directions

This selection is approximately 1¹/2 minutes long. It is important to be sure you understand the passage before practicing repeating. Take time to study and understand the passage first. Answer the comprehension questions in ASL. Recording your answers to the comprehension questions is optional. Complete the repetition and answer the study questions. You will need a quiet place to work where you will not be interrupted and where you can record your repetition and responses. Record yourself while you are engaged in immediate repetition. Begin repeating as soon as the selection on the DVD starts. After you finish your repetition, review your work and record your answers to the study questions in ASL. Remember, during this exercise you are not required to remember what you repeat. Be sure to study the passage first.

Comprehension Questions

1. What is the name of the group he belongs to?

2. Who are the members of this group?

3. What does this group do for its members?

4. How does this organization help students stay in school and graduate?

5. Study the fingerspelled words. The list shown below provides the English translation of the fingerspelled words. Play the fingerspelled words at least five times until you are sure you can easily recognize each word.

English Translations of Fingerspelled Words:
  Union
  Campus
  Howard

Study Questions

1. Were you able to concentrate on the segmenting incoming information? Think about how your mind organizes the information into segments. As you continue practicing, become more aware of how your mind segments information into idea units.

2. Were you able to monitor your own output while repeating? Was your repetition accurate? Circle the word below that best describes how difficult it was for you to monitor your own output during repetition.

   Very difficult   Difficult   Easy

3. Did you find that your signing distracted you or that your signing was not accurate as you continued to watch the source? Circle the word below that best describes how distracted you were by your own signing during repetition

   Very distracted   Somewhat distracted   Not distracted

4. Were you able to gain control of the your processing time in order to keep a short processing time in effect throughout the repetition?

5. What kinds of things distracted you? Some examples could include your own signing, noise in the room, other visual noise? How did you filter these distractions out so that you could continue repeating?

Repeat the exercise and see whether your ASL is more understandable the second time. Does the syntax of your repetition better match the speaker's?

EXERCISE 4.3

Honey-Glazed Carrots

JESSICA OLSEN-DUNBAR

Directions

This selection is approximately 1 1/2 minutes long. It is important to be sure you understand the passage before practicing repeating. Take time to study and understand the passage first. Answer the comprehension questions in ASL. Recording your answers to the comprehension questions is optional. Complete the repetition and answer the study questions. You will need a quiet place to work where you will not be interrupted and where you can record your repetition and responses. Record yourself while you are engaged in immediate repetition. Begin repeating as soon as the selection on the DVD starts. After you finish your repetition, review your work and record your answers to the study questions in ASL. Remember, during this exercise you are not required to remember what you repeat. Be sure to study the passage first.

Comprehension Questions

1. What does this sign mean in this context?

01:48:23;00

2. Paraphrase this sentence.

01:48:44;23 to 01:48:52;22

3. What does the space to the left of the signer represent?

4. What holidays does she refer to?

5. Study the fingerspelled words. The list shown below provides the English translation of the fingerspelled words. Play the fingerspelled words at least five times until you are sure you can easily recognize each word.

   English Translations of Fingerspelled Words:
   Recipe
   Honey-glazed carrots
   Pounds (lbs)
   Inch
   Steam
   Cup
   Stick
   Cinnamon (cinn) and nutmeg

Study Questions

1. Were you able to concentrate on the segmenting incoming information? Think about how your mind organizes the information into segments.

2. Were you able to monitor your own output while repeating? Was your repetition accurate?

3. Did you find that your signing distracted you or that your signing was not accurate as you continued to watch the source?

4. Were you able to gain control of the your processing time in order to keep a short processing time in effect throughout the repletion?

5. What kinds of things distracted you? Some examples could include your own signing, noise in the room, other visual noise? How did you filter these distractions out so that you could continue repeating?

Repeat the exercise and see whether your ASL is more understandable the second time. Does the syntax of your repetition better match the speaker's?

Progress Tracking Sheet

A progress tracking sheet is at the end of each unit. This sheet is designed to help you keep track of which exercises you have completed and how well you have done on these exercises. A rating system is presented for you to rate the outcomes of your work on the exercises. After completing each exercise and activity, fill in the tracking sheet. Your instructor may ask you to copy and submit the tracking sheet for each unit. Rate your performance on the exercises using the following scale: excellent (no serious errors) = 5 points; good (some errors, but not serious) = 4 points; fair (many errors, some serious) = 3 points; not satisfactory (many errors, most are serious) = 2 points; poor (missed the point of the exercise—must redo) =1 point.

Exercise Number and Name	Date	First Performance Rating	Second Performance Rating	Questions and Reminders
Exercise 4.1 Autobiography				
Exercise 4.2 My Involvement in Black Deaf Student Union				
Exercise 4.3 Honey-Glazed Carrots				

UNIT 5

Delayed Repetition

Throughout this book the emphasis is on learning about and practicing the cognitive skills that form a basis for simultaneous interpreting. Studying the parts of a more complex task is called "part-task training" by De Groot (1997) who explains that a number of studies have shown that training in the components of a complex process does transfer to effective performance of the whole task, in this case, simultaneous interpreting. De Groot also points out that the most unique feature of simultaneous interpreting is its requirement of simultaneity of comprehension and production. During interpreting this process is interlingual, but during the practice of repetition or delayed repetition the comprehension and production of a message is within a language.

After immediate repetition skills are in place, it is important to add the skill of delayed repetition. Delayed repetition means repetition that begins after an enforced waiting period. That waiting period could be a very brief time interval or it could be an interval based on a unit of information such as a phrase (Lambert, 1989). By adding a delay to the repetition process, the foundations for gaining control of decalage, processing time, or lag time can be enhanced. Decalage, processing time, lag time, and ear–voice span all refer to the same thing: the amount of time that elapses between the moment that the interpreter hears the message and the moment that the interpreter interprets that message.

The ability to perform delayed repetition at the phrase level indicates the ability to segment incoming messages into component parts or phrases. Delayed-repetition ability forms the basis for developing processing time during simultaneous interpreting. It is important to be able to find the natural breaks in signed ASL to be able to effectively use processing time while interpreting.

Although delayed repetition requires the use of both long-term memory and working memory or short-term memory, a heavier emphasis is placed on short term memory processing. Flaws in short-term memory processing lead to an increase in errors in interpreting. Short term memory stores are thought to be approximately 15 to 30 seconds (Carroll, 2005).

In general, more effort will be required for delayed repetition than immediate repetition. This is especially true if the receiver is not familiar with the procedures or propositions in the text. The ability to successfully manage delayed repetition indicates the ability to effectively use the following: attending to signing, finding phrases, monitoring phrasal distance, signing while watching, and monitoring output of the repetition. All of these abilities are important components of the interpreting process.

The Role of Delayed Repetition in the Interpreting Process

The ability to use processing time effectively is an essential and important part of the interpreting process. The ability to repeat with a delay is one aspect of training in simultaneous interpreting. Ingram (1984) described processing time this way:

> To lag, or in simultaneous interpreting, it refers to the span of time between the interpreter's perception of the source language and the subsequent production of the target language rendition. It is the period of time between the interpreter's input and output.

Interpreters with greater control of decalage skills tend to make fewer errors (Lambert, 1989, p. 49).

Cokely (1986) studied four interpreters to analyze the effect of processing time on the number of errors or miscues while interpreting. He found that interpreters who could use the longest amount of processing time tended to make fewer errors. He analyzed various types of errors, including omissions, additions, substitutions, intrusions, and anomalies. When all types of errors were grouped, the interpreters in the Cokely study who used a 2-second processing time made more than twice as many errors as those who used a 4-second processing time. Those who used a 4-second processing time made twice as many errors as those who used a 6-second processing time. Cokely summarizes the results of his study by saying, "The greater lag time, the more information available; the more information available, the greater the level of comprehension" (p. 67). Another way to see the importance of gaining control over delayed repetition as a stepping-stone to strong interpreting skills is to look at Gile's (1995) *Effort Model of Interpreting.* He provides a formula that shows that simultaneous interpreting requires effort in three main areas that are described briefly below. In the context of the simultaneous interpreting process we can see that the Memory Effort is essential to the simultaneous interpreting process.

Formula: **SI = L + M + P**

SI = *Simultaneous Interpreting*

L = *Listening and Analysis,* which includes "all the mental operations between perception of a discourse by auditory mechanisms and the moment at which the interpreter either assigns, or decides not to assign, a meaning (or several potential meanings) to the segment which he has heard."

M = *Short-term Memory,* which includes "all the mental operations related to storage in memory of heard segments of discourse until either their restitution in the target language, their loss if they vanish from memory, or a decision by the interpreter not to interpret them."

P = *Production,* which includes "all the mental operations between the moment at which the interpreter decides to convey a datum or an idea and the moment at which he articulates (overtly produces) the form he has prepared to articulate"

One way to improve your short-term memory skills is to practice delayed repetition exercises.

The importance of being able to use processing time well in the interpretation process cannot be overstated. Delayed repetition in the interpreter's L2 is an essential building block for developing processing time during the interpreting process.

EXERCISES IN DELAYED REPETITION

EXERCISE 5.1

Easy Lasagna

ELIZABETH CREAMER

Directions

This exercise has two selections. The first short segment allows you to get to know the signer and become accustomed to her signing style and the second segment allows you to focus on delayed repetition skills.

The second selection is approximately 3 1/2 minutes long. It is important to be sure you understand the passage before practicing repeating. Take time to study and understand the passage first. Answer the comprehension questions in ASL. Record and review them to examine your ASL production. Respond to the study questions as directed.

Find this selection on your DVD. You will need to video record yourself while you are engaged in delayed repetition. Begin repeating 4 seconds after the selection has started. There is a visual signal provided on the DVD to let you know when the first 4 seconds have elapsed. Wait until you see that signal. There will be no additional signals during the rest of the passage. Try to keep a processing time of 4 seconds or a phrase length behind the signer as you continue your repetition. It is normal to vary the amount of processing time as you continue through the passage but try to keep the processing time as long as possible.

After completing the repetition, review your work and record your answers to the study questions.

Get to Know the Signer

This short segment allows you to get acquainted with the signer and is about 2 minutes long. Watch the selection and replay it until you can answer the following questions. Respond in ASL. You do not need to record your responses.

1. Where is Elizabeth from?

_____

2. How many generations of deafness in her family so far?

_____

3. Are her parents deaf?

_____

4. How many siblings in her family and how many of them are deaf?

_____

5. How many nieces and nephews are there and how many are deaf?

_____

6. Where does Elizabeth work?

_____

Comprehension Questions

1. What does this sign mean in this context?

01:50:24;05

2. How long does it take to cook it?

3. What type of baking utensils do you need?

4. How much water do you need?

5. How do you prepare the pan?

6. How many noodles do you need?

7. What kind of meat do you need?

8. How do you layer the ingredients?

9. What do these signs mean in this context?

01:53:19;22 to 01:53:27;20

10. What do you cover the pan with before baking?

11. How long does it need to bake?

12. Study the fingerspelled words. The list shown below provides the English translation of the fingerspelled words. Play the fingerspelled words at least five times until you are sure you can easily recognize each word.

   English Translations of Fingerspelled Words:
   Pan
   Pot
   Oil
   Noodles (spelled nooles)
   Ground beef
   Ground turkey
   Drain
   Done
   Layer
   Season
   Oregano
   Basil leave
   Sauce
   Ricotta cheese
   Mozzarella (moz) cheese
   It
   Aluminum (alum) foil

Oven

Bake

All

Meal

Study Questions

These study questions are designed to help you gain insight into the efforts used in the delayed repetition process. These are some of the same efforts you will be using later in simultaneous interpreting.

1. We can adapt the Listening and Analysis Effort in Gile's Effort Model to comprehending a signed message. Think about the ease and rapidity with which you comprehended the ASL source message during delayed repetition.

   How difficult was it for you to comprehend ASL and keep going in the repetition process? Circle the word that best describes how difficult it seemed to you.

   Very Difficult   Difficult   Easy

2. Adapting the second part of Gile's Effort Model, the Short Term Memory Effort, to remembering the incoming ASL as you practiced repetition, think about how easy or difficult it was for you to remember the ASL that you saw long enough to reproduce it.

   How difficult was it for you to remember the incoming ASL and keep going in the repetition process? Circle the word that best describes how difficult it seemed to you.

   Very Difficult   Difficult   Easy

3. Adapting the third effort, Production, from Gile's Effort Model think about the process during which you decide which signs to convey and then convey them during repetition.

   How difficult was it for you to remember the incoming ASL and keep going in the repetition process? Circle the word that best describes how difficult it seemed to you.

   Very Difficult   Difficult   Easy

EXERCISE 5.2

Alaska Adventure

STEVE SANDY

Directions

This exercise has two selections. The first short segment allows you to get to know the signer and become accustomed to his signing style and the second segment allows you to focus on delayed repetition skills.

The second selection is approximately 3 minutes long. It is important to be sure you understand the passage before practicing repeating. Take time to study and understand the passage first. Answer the comprehension questions in ASL and record your answers. Be sure to use complete sentences following ASL syntax. Answer the comprehension questions as directed.

Try to keep a processing time 4 seconds or a phrase length behind the signer as you continue your repetition.

It is normal to vary the amount of processing time as you continue through the passage but try to keep the processing time as long as possible.

After completing the repetition, review your repetition and answers to the comprehension questions. Answer the study questions as directed.

Find this selection on your DVD. You will need to video record yourself while you are engaged in delayed repetition. Begin repeating 4 seconds after the selection has started. There is a visual signal provided on the DVD to let you know when the first 4 seconds have elapsed. Wait until you see that signal. There will be no additional signals during the rest of the passage. Try to keep a processing time of 4 seconds or a phrase length behind the signer as you continue your repetition.

After completing the repetition, review your repetition and answers to the comprehension questions and answer the study questions.

Get to Know the Signer

This short segment allows you to get acquainted with the signer and is about 2 minutes long. Watch the selection and replay it until you can answer the following questions. Respond in ASL. You do not need to record your responses.

1. Was Steve born deaf?

2.　What is the cause of his deafness?

_____

_____

3.　Are there other family members who are deaf?

_____

4.　Has he traveled all the way around the world?

_____

5.　Where was he born?

_____

6.　Where has he lived?

_____

Comprehension Questions

1.　When did he live in Alaska?

2.　What kind of fish was he hoping to catch on his fishing trip?

3.　Who went on the fishing trip?

4.　What does this sign mean in this context?

01:55:11;06

5. Paraphrase this part of the selection.

01:55:07;15 to 01:55:17;19

6. Did Steve catch fish? Look for the negation.

7. What does this sign mean in this context?

01:55:34;23

8. Paraphrase this part of the selection.

01:55:36;20 to 01:55:40;18

9. Paraphrase this part of the selection.

01:55:41;18 to 01:55:52;22

10. What happened when Steve was looking at the fish that the man had caught?

11. What did Steve want to avoid?

12. How did he try to solve the problem?

13. In this part of the selection, what happened to Steve?

01:56:13;20 to 01:56:17;28

14. How much daylight is there in Alaska in the winter?

15. What do these signs mean in this context?

01:56:50;10 to 01:56:52;24

16. What do these signs mean in this context?

01:56:55;23 to 01:57:02;25

17. Paraphrase this part of the selection.

01:57:13;03 to 01:57:24;10

18. Paraphrase this part of the selection.

01:57:27;00 to 01:57:32;13

19. When did his mother take his picture?

20. Paraphrase this part of the selection?

01:57:50;24 to 01:57:55;26

21. Study the fingerspelled words. The list shown below provides the English translation of the fingerspelled words. Play the fingerspelled words at least five times until you are sure you can easily recognize each word.

English Translations of Fingerspelled Words:
Alaska

Air Force

Trip

Denali (spelled Denli)

Sir

Unusual

State fair

Big

Cabbage

Cucumbers

Study Questions

These study questions are designed to help you gain insight into the efforts used in the delayed repetition process. These are some of the same efforts you will be using later in simultaneous interpreting. Notice how the increased length of this selection affected your work and your insights into your process.

1. We can adapt the Listening and Analysis Effort in Gile's Effort Model to comprehending a signed message. Think about the ease and rapidity with which you comprehended the ASL source message during delayed repetition.

    How difficult was it for you to comprehend ASL and keep going in the repetition process? Circle the word that best describes how difficult it seemed to you.

    Very Difficult   Difficult   Easy

2. Adapting the second part of Gile's Effort Model, the Short Term Memory Effort, to remembering the incoming ASL as you practiced repetition, think about how easy or difficult it was for you to remember the ASL that you saw long enough to reproduce it.

   How difficult was it for you to remember the incoming ASL and keep going in the repetition process? Circle the word that best describes how difficult it seemed to you.

   Very Difficult   Difficult   Easy

3. Adapting the third effort, Production, from Gile's Effort Model think about the process during which you decide which signs to convey and then convey them during repetition.

   How difficult was it for you to remember the incoming ASL and keep going in the repetition process? Circle the word that best describes how difficult it seemed to you.

   Very Difficult   Difficult   Easy

EXERCISE 5.3

More Hot Peppers

BARBARA BUCHANAN

Directions

This exercise has two selections. The first short segment allows you to get to know the signer and become accustomed to her signing style and the second segment allows you to focus on delayed repetition skills.

The second selection is approximately 3 1/2 minutes long. It is important to be sure you understand the passage before practicing repeating. Take time to study and understand the passage first. Record your answers to the comprehension questions. Use complete sentences following ASL syntax.

Find this selection on your DVD. You will need to video record yourself while you are engaged in delayed repetition. Begin repeating 4 seconds after the selection has started. There is a visual signal provided on the DVD to let you know when the first 4 seconds have elapsed. Wait until you see that signal. There will be no additional signals during the rest of the passage. Try to keep a processing time of 4 seconds or a phrase length behind the signer as you continue your repetition.

After completing the repetition, review your repetition and answers to the comprehension questions, then answer the study questions. Remember, during this exercise you are not required to remember what you repeat. Be sure to study the passage first.

Get to Know the Signer

This short segment allows you to get acquainted with the signer and is about 2 minutes long. Watch the selection and replay it until you can answer the following questions. Respond in ASL. You do not need to record your responses.

1. Where did she grow up?

   _____

2. Where does she live now?

   _____

3. When did she become deaf?

   _____

Comprehension Questions

1. Is this a true story?

2. When did she move to San Diego?

3. What kinds of plants did her friend have in the garden?

4. What did she want to do with the peppers?

5. Did she want to freeze the peppers whole?

6. What was the bad experience she had when she froze peppers in the past?

7. How did she solve the problem with her hands?

8.   Did she learn a lesson from her previous experience with peppers?

9.   When her friend invited her to eat jalapeño peppers was she eager to eat them?

10. How did her friend respond to her refusal to eat the peppers?

11. What kind of peppers were being served and were they very hot?

12. What did she do, just to be polite?

13. What does this sign mean in this context?

02:00:56;16

14. What does this sign mean in this context?

02:01:05;18

15. What did she tell her friend?

16. What did her friend do to help solve the problem?

17. Did the vitamin E oil help her?

18. What does she plan to do?

19. Study the fingerspelled words. The list shown below provides the English translation of the fingerspelled words. Play the fingerspelled words at least five times until you are sure you can easily recognize each word.

English Translations of Fingerspelled Words:

Garden (spelled gaden)

Peppers

Jalapeño

What to do with them

Chili

Stem off

Seeds

Ice

No

OK

Firecracker

Oil

Burn

Vitamin E oil (vit)

Study Questions

These study questions are designed to help you gain insight into the efforts used in the delayed repetition process. These are some of the same efforts you will be using later in simultaneous interpreting.

1. We can adapt the Listening and Analysis Effort in Gile's Effort Model to comprehending a signed message. Think about the ease and rapidity with which you comprehended the ASL source message during delayed repetition.

   How difficult was it for you to comprehend ASL and keep going in the repetition process? Circle the word that best describes how difficult it seemed to you.

   Very Difficult   Difficult   Easy

2. Adapting the second part of Gile's Effort Model, the Short Term Memory Effort, to remembering the incoming ASL as you practiced repetition, think about how easy or difficult it was for you to remember the ASL that you saw long enough to reproduce it.

How difficult was it for you to remember the incoming ASL and keep going in the repetition process? Circle the word that best describes how difficult it seemed to you.

Very Difficult   Difficult   Easy

3. Adapting the third effort, Production, from Gile's Effort Model think about the process during which you decide which signs to convey and then convey them during repetition.

How difficult was it for you to remember the incoming ASL and keep going in the repetition process? Circle the word that best describes how difficult it seemed to you.

Very Difficult   Difficult   Easy

Progress Tracking Sheet

A progress tracking sheet is at the end of each unit. This sheet is designed to help you keep track of which exercises you have completed and how well you have done on these exercises. A rating system is presented for you to rate the outcomes of your work on the exercises. After completing each exercise and activity, fill in the tracking sheet. Your instructor may ask you to copy and submit the tracking sheet for each unit. Rate your performance on the exercises using the following scale: excellent (no serious errors) = 5 points; good (some errors, but not serious) = 4 points; fair (many errors, some serious) = 3 points; not satisfactory (many errors, most are serious) = 2 points; poor (missed the point of the exercise—must redo) =1 point.

Exercise Number and Name	Date	First Performance Rating	Second Performance Rating	Questions and Reminders
Exercise 5.1 Easy Lasagna				
Exercise 5.2 Alaska Adventrue				
Exercise 5.3 More Hot Peppers				

UNIT 6

Fingerspelled Word Recognition and Comprehension of Numbers in ASL

Unit 6 provides an introduction to developing cognitive strategies needed for comprehending ASL that includes fingerspelled word recognition and ASL number recognition. These two topics are often treated together but in reality require different skill sets for successful comprehension. Reading fingerspelled words requires lexical access to the word that the fingerspelling represents which is a more complex task than number recognition. Sign language interpreters are acutely aware, more so than other signers, of the difficulty in correctly recognizing fingerspelled words. Although it may not be immediately apparent, there may be underlying deficiencies in individuals' specific skills that hinder correct recognition of the fingerspelled word. Many errors in ASL-to-English interpretations are caused by weaknesses in comprehending lexical items in ASL, including fingerspelled word recognition (Taylor, 2002). The interpreting process requires simultaneously managing a wide range of enormously demanding cognitive, linguistic, and interpersonal tasks. However, without strong comprehension skills, the interpreting process cannot even begin.

Fingerspelled Word Recognition in Interpreting

Many interpreters report that fingerspelled word recognition is both difficult and anxiety producing. Alternatively, other interpreters report that finger-spelled word recognition is not problematic (Patrie, 1989). The individuals are usually experienced interpreters who find that reading fingerspelled words is no different from reading other aspects of sign language. Their success can be attributed to the development of specific strategies that are appropriate to fingerspelled word recognition.

Hearing individuals learning ASL as adults generally have great difficulty in correctly recognizing fingerspelled words. This difficulty hampers their ability to fully comprehend signed messages, leads to misunderstanding and frustra-tion, and can delay them in developing comprehension in ASL. Producing fin-gerspelled words is challenging as well, but this task tends to pale in comparison to the difficulty of accurately recognizing them. I have collected data and con-ducted research over the last 20 years with the goal of helping interpreters im-prove fingerspelled word recognition to reduce the widespread anxiety commonly associated with reading fingerspelled words. This unit summarizes some of the important aspects of my research and provides information and ex-ercises to help improve your fingerspelled word recognition skills.

How Anxiety Affects Fingerspelled Word Recognition

Failure to recognize the fingerspelled word in context on the first try leads to a variety of problems, such as the immediate loss of confidence. Even after the fingerspelled word is repeated, it is often still not understood, leading to increased anxiety and a breakdown in the comprehension process. You may not recognize the fingerspelled word when it is repeated because it is usually spelled more slowly or carefully the second time and because it will not look exactly the same as it did the first time. You may feel even more frustrated or anxious because you think that you should be even better able to understand the word on the second try.

You may have had negative experiences related to failures in fingerspelled word recognition. This common experience adds an emotional component, on top of the presence of anxiety, to the difficult cognitive task of fingerspelled word recognition. The emotion you experienced during an event becomes a hard-wired part of the memory of that event. If you have anxious feelings as you learned to recognize or attempt to recognize fingerspelled words, the anxiety remains a part of that memory trace.

Because anxiety is activated by earlier attempts at fingerspelled word recog-nition, anxiety is automatically reactivated each time a fingerspelled word ap-pears. Novice signers report that they feel nervous or anxious just *thinking* about reading fingerspelled words and that they want to avoid reading them so they will not feel embarrassed. Likewise, these novices often avoid expressing them-selves using fingerspelling to avoid the possibility of a fingerspelled response.

Most people who have difficulty reading fingerspelled words also try to avoid fingerspelling. The combination leads to an overall aversion to finger-spelled words, whether produced or read.

The pervasive anxiety associated with fingerspelled word recognition can be attributed to the many prevailing beliefs and strategies that are either erroneous or ineffective and can easily lead to anxiety, rather than success. Gillory's 1966 text, despite its advanced age, is still regarded as landmark text and is widely used in sign language classes for hearing adults. This text, and others like it, lacks a sequential approach to fingerspelling that explains the cognitive differences between expressive and receptive fingerspelling.

Many ASL begin their study of sign language in classes conducted with an emphasis on expression rather than comprehension of the language. Ordinarily, it is best to learn to comprehend a language before being expected to use the language expressively. It is not unusual to meet ASL and interpreting students who are not able to understand signs and fingerspelling as well as they can produce them. This expressive-first approach to learning ASL makes it difficult for sign language students and prospective interpreters to make systematic and satisfying progress in fingerspelled word recognition skills. Perhaps the overlooked central issue is that fingerspelled word recognition is a visual recognition task, and that special visual training is especially required for hearing adults who want to learn ASL as a second language.

There are many prevailing beliefs and strategies that have created myths and misconceptions about the nature of the fingerspelled word. These prevailing beliefs and strategies are widely held as truths even though they have no basis in experimental science. These erroneous beliefs and strategies are so pervasive that they may have a negative influence on the ability to comprehend new approaches to dealing with fingerspelled words. These erroneous beliefs lead to strategies are either not true, not effective, or both. Using effective strategies leads to more effective perceptions of the facts surrounding fingerspelled words.

Fingerspelled word recognition can be the most difficult aspect of ASL comprehension. Yet it is critical to accurate understanding of ASL, and of particular importance to second language learners who aspire to easily interact with signers in conversation and in professional contexts. Specific avenues to improvement include studying the nature of the fingerspelled word and direct practice in reading fingerspelled words through a process of developing templates or word recognition patterns.

Templates in Fingerspelled Word Recognition

It may *seem* that the fingerspelled word is either "seen" or processed as a single unitary event by adept individuals. In fact, the processing of fingerspelled words is far more complex than that and may depend on the experiences and methods used by the individual in developing recognition strategies. Successful readers of fingerspelled words probably use a combination of strategies including sequential processing and template or pattern creation and matching, as well as pattern inference. The templates are for the printed form of the word and/or the fingerspelled form of the word. Both of these types of templates access the meaning of the word. The more experienced fingerspelled reader is more likely to access the meaning of the word directly from the fingerspelled template. Less experienced readers may access the template for the written word and then the meaning of the word. The perceptual event of fingerspelled words is a sequential task because "[e]ach symbol is presented for a brief time, generally in the same physical position, and in that sequence forms a word" (Zakia, 1972). Second language learners of ASL must develop the cognitive sub-skill of rapidly processing serially presented information.

Successful readers of fingerspelled words do not consciously realize that they use these strategies; they experience successfully recognizing the fingerspelled word. Recognition is achieved by combining a variety of skills that allow a 'gestalt' or recognition all-at-once sensation. If you have built a template for a fingerspelled word, then you feel as if you have seen the whole word at once even though you actually perceived the word serially.

Template Building

It is possible to develop expertise in fingerspelled word recognition only through deliberate and appropriate practice over time. Effective practice methods and self-confidence are also essential to recognizing fingerspelled words. One aspect of developing fingerspelled word recognition skills is template building. If you can easily read print, you have already built many templates used for print word recognition. The templates for printed words (the easy recognition of printed words) form a strong foundation for creating templates for fingerspelled words. In effect, learning to recognize the pattern of handshapes in a fingerspelled word will eventually activate templates for both the written word and the fingerspelled word. Eventually, with enough appropriate practice, the fingerspelled word itself will activate access to the meaning.

My research has shown that the quickest, most effective way to build a template for a fingerspelled word is to watch the word in context and study the same word in slow motion, regular speed, slow motion and then again in context. It is necessary to repeat this process at least five times to have a strong pattern for the word created in your memory.

Successful readers of fingerspelled words have developed their own pattern recognition strategies through repeated exposures to the fingerspelled word. Through repetition, successful fingerspelled word readers are able to recognize the fingerspelled word on the first try. When this recognition happens that person has established and stored a pattern or "template" for that word in their visual memory. Visual events should be encoded visually, not via auditory mechanisms such as pronouncing the names of the corresponding character from the Roman alphabet as you see the corresponding signs appear in the word.

Successful readers of fingerspelled words are not recognizing the shape of the word. In fact, it is impossible to recognize the shape of a fingerspelled word. Fingerspelled words do not have a static shape that can be reinspected like a printed word could. Fingerspelled words appear one letter at a time not as an entire shape that can be seen all at once. It is possible to recognize and recall the cumulative dynamic movement patterns within the word, but it is misleading to refer to these characteristics as shapes or outlines. The fingerspelled word is a dynamic event, not static. After a template for the fingerspelled word (or the printed word) has been established through practice and encoded visually, you can rapidly access the equivalent English word.

An example of the template building process was developed by Patrie (1997) in *Fingerspelled Names and Introductions: A Template Building Approach.* Viewers report that this specific series of types of presentations improves fingerspelled word recognition. This successful technique has been adapted for the DVD that accompanies this study set.

Numbers in the Interpretation Process

Moser-Mercer (1983), who uses the term "processing" of numbers, suggests that numbers are notoriously problematic for interpreters. Moser-Mercer says that the processing of numbers requires the accurate preservation of exact numeral information in running discourse. She says, "From a language information processing point of view, the processing of numbers differs from that of continuous text, in that numbers are largely unpredictable" (p. 59) and require something like a sudden shifting of gears. This means that the context does not increase the interpreter's chances of correctly filling in the blank if the number is missed.

Pattern inference skills are not likely to help the interpreter decide what number could fill in the blank. For example, if an interpreter hears the following sentence fragment "The cost of the house will be _____," there is no way for the interpreter to be able to correctly fill in the blank because of the unpredictability of numbers.

Lambert (1989) points out that "digits have meaning only when associated with words, and they are highly unpredictable" (p. 51). She suggests that the difficulty may be caused by the possibility that digits are processed differently than the rest of the message, perhaps involving a switch in cerebral dominance. Gile (1995) says that numbers are likely to cause problems for interpreters, not because they require a great deal of processing capacity, but because numbers are a more "vulnerable" signal. By this, Gile means that numbers are short in duration and low in redundancy. Another way to look at Gile's idea is to realize that the name of the number does not take long to say and is usually not repeated. Gile goes on to say that the numerical information can be lost during even a brief lapse of attention. Once the number has been missed because of poor attention strategies or forgotten because of poor memory strategies, it is quite likely that the entire interpretation process can break down at that point. The exercises in Unit 6 focus on improving comprehension of fingerspelled words and numbers in context.

The exercises in Unit 6 focus on comprehension of fingerspelled words and numbers. The "Get to Know the Signer" sections help student to become acquainted with the signers' style.

EXERCISES FOR FINGERSPELLED WORD RECOGNITION AND NUMBERS

EXERCISE 6.1

The Football Pool

VAUGHN HALLADA

Directions

This exercise has two selections. The first short segment allows you to get to know the signer and become accustomed to his signing style and the second segment allows you to focus on fingerspelling and number recognition.

The second selection is approximately 6 minutes long. Study the passage several times, using slow motion wherever necessary. When you feel confident that you have understood the passage, answer the comprehension questions in ASL using complete sentences. Record your answers.

Get to Know the Signer

This short segment allows you to get acquainted with the signer and is about 2 minutes long. Watch the selection and replay it until you can answer the following questions. Respond in ASL. You do not need to record your responses.

1. What town is Vaughn from?

   _____

2. What does his town look like?

   _____

3. How long does he plan to live there?

   _____

   _____

4. What does Vaughn do for a living?

   _____

5. How long has he been teaching there?

   _____

Comprehension Questions

1. What is the first rule?

2. What are examples of what you should do?

3. What kinds of things can work against you in your bet?

4. Where is the football pool determined?

5. Why do people lose money in the football pool?

6. Study the fingerspelled words. The list shown below provides the English translation of the fingerspelled words. Play the fingerspelled words at least five times until you are sure you can easily recognize each word.

   ### English Translations of Fingerspelled Words:

   Pool

   Do

   Ranking

   Las Vegas (LV)

   Sports book

   Mafia (spelled mafa)

   Costa Rica

   Green Bay

   Steelers

   Denver

   San Diego (SD)

   Palm trees

   Don't

   Even

   New York Giants (NY)

   TV

   NHL

Coach
NBA
Lakers
By
Los Angeles (LA)
Away

7. Correct recognition of numbers is an essential skill for interpreters. In this clip, several ideas or sentences will show that include a number. Play the selection several times until you can easily recognize each number. After you can easily recognize the numbers, turn on your recording device and sign each number, using it in a new sentence.

3 1/2

7 1/2

38

21

14

35

50

100

200

500

350

1

2

3

4

5

10

70

4 1/2

11

25

_____

_____

EXERCISE 6.2

Numbers in ASL

MINNIE MAE WILDING-DIAZ

Directions

This exercise has two selections. The first short segment allows you to get to know the signer and become accustomed to her signing style and the second segment allows you to focus on fingerspelling and number recognition.

The second selection is approximately 4 minutes long. Study the passage several times, using slow motion wherever necessary. When you feel confident that you have understood the passage, answer the comprehension questions in ASL using complete sentences. Record your answers.

Get to Know the Signer

This short segment allows you to get acquainted with the signer and is about 2 minutes long. Watch the selection and replay it until you can answer the following questions. Respond in ASL. You do not need to record your responses.

1. Where does she live?

_____

2. Who in her family is deaf?

_____

_____

Comprehension Questions

1. What is her pet peeve?

2. What does Minnie Mae say the palm orientation should be for numbers 1 through 5?

3. What is the exception to the palm facing outward for numbers 1 through 5?

4. What are her instructions for numbers 6 through 9?

5. How do you indicate height?

6. Study the fingerspelled words. The list shown below provides the English translation of the fingerspelled words. Play the fingerspelled words at least five times until you are sure you can easily recognize each word.

    ### English Translations of Fingerspelled Words:
    Mini

    Pet peeve

    Social security number (SS)

7. Correct recognition of numbers is an essential skill for interpreters. In this clip, several ideas or sentences will show that include a number. Play the selection several times until you can easily recognize each number. After you can easily recognize the numbers, turn on your recording device and sign each number, using it in a new sentence.

    2

    1

    3

    4

    5

    6

    7

    8

    10

    12

    15

    20

    35

    40

    50

    Age 1, 2, 3

    1, 2, 3 o'clock

    12268

    373–5585

3 children

2 cars

5'1"

5'8"

5'7"

6'5"

7'5"

7'2"

EXERCISE 6.3

My Drive to Work

VAUGHN HALLADA

Directions

This passage is 3 minutes long and should be assigned for out-of-class study. Use in-class time for discussion and questions, as well as checking student responses.

This passage is about 3 minutes long. Study the passage several times, using slow motion wherever necessary. When you feel confident that you have understood the passage, answer the comprehension questions in ASL using complete sentences. Record your answers.

Comprehension Questions

1. Where does he work and what is it near?

2. What is the name of his town and where is it located?

3. Summarize the route he takes to work.

4. Study the fingerspelled words. The list shown below provides the English translation of the fingerspelled words. Play the fingerspelled words at least five times until you are sure you can easily recognize each word.

   English Translations of Fingerspelled Words:
   Michigan (Mich)
   Port Washington

Wisconsin (Wis)

Green Bay

Mississippi River (spelled Mispi)

Lake

Silver Spring

Good Hope

5. Correct recognition of numbers is an essential skill for interpreters. In this clip, several ideas or sentences will show that include a number. Play the selection several times until you can easily recognize each number. After you can easily recognize the numbers, turn on your recording device and sign each number, using it in a new sentence.

Highway 32

I–43

5:30

4

18

7 minutes

6th floor

681

680

8 o'clock

Progress Tracking Sheet

A progress tracking sheet is provided at the end of each unit. This sheet is designed to help you keep track of which exercises you have completed and how well you have done on these exercises. A rating system is presented for you to rate the outcomes of your work on the exercises. After completing each exercise and activity, fill in the tracking sheet. Your instructor may ask you to copy and submit the tracking sheet for each unit. Rate your performance on the exercises using the following scale: excellent (no serious errors) = 5 points; good (some errors, but not serious) = 4 points; fair (many errors, some serious) = 3 points; not satisfactory (many errors, most are serious) = 2 points; poor (missed the point of the exercise—must redo) =1 point.

Exercise Number and Name	Date	First Performance Rating	Second Performance Rating	Questions and Reminders
Exercise 6.1 The Football Pool				
Exercise 6.2 Numbers in ASL				
Exercise 6.3 My Drive to Work				

UNIT

7

Pattern Inference in ASL

Pattern inference when used in reference to language proficiency is the ability to complete a pattern within a language based on the context provided. Another way to think of this concept is filling in the blank in a sentence with a sign that makes sense in that context. In Unit 7, pattern inference drills are those in which a sign is deleted and the viewer must fill in the missing sign with a sign that makes sense in that context.

Historically, interpreter education borrowed the word cloze from the field of *reading comprehension* and used it to mean a specific form of language proficiency other than that for which it was originally intended. Typically, cloze drills are written materials in which every 5th to 10th word is deleted. (Oller, 1988). To fill in the missing word, the reader of the written passage must have a good enough knowledge of the language and strong enough reading comprehension skills to know which word would logically fit in the blank without changing the meaning of the sentence. If the reader can do this, the reader knows the patterns of the language well enough to fill in the missing words. The ability to fill in a missing word when reading can be an indicator of reading proficiency. However, in interpreting we are not reading print, but processing spoken or signed messages. Interpreters working between ASL and English must develop skills within each language as it is used in real time, not in a printed form. As interpreters, we are often required to fill in a word or sign when we could not fully hear or see the original message. This "filling in" process or pattern inference is a valuable professional tool, if it is used correctly. In Unit 7, we explore the importance of pattern inference and how it relates to interpreting. Unit 7 describes word-level pattern inference and phrase-level pattern inference.

Word-Level Pattern Inference

In interpreter education programs, this kind of "missing word" drill often appears as a spoken language drill and is used to develop linguistic abilities that are needed in the interpreting process. Pattern inference skills can be demonstrated at two different levels. One level is grammatical. At this level you ask yourself which sign or kind of sign would make sense in the blank. Sometimes the blank can be filled in with only one sign and other times a variety of signs will make sense. The important point here is that the blank must be filled in with a sign or combination of signs that makes sense in context.

Phrase-Level Pattern Inference

The presence of pattern inference skills at the grammatical level means that the receiver has enough linguistic skill to make logical inferences as to which sign or signs could reasonably be used to complete an idea. Phrase-level pattern inference can also be called pattern completion skills. It is important to stress that completing linguistic patterns is not based on guesswork, but rather on knowledge of ASL and how the patterns of ASL are typically expressed. Pattern inference skills are valuable in training and in the real world of interpreting. By relying on context and having strong language skills, especially comprehension, you will know which signs could make sense in a specific context.

These pattern completion skills are based on having strong linguistic skills and on being able to use context to find possible and logical solutions. Pattern inference skills at the phrase level form another subset of skills that are necessary for both interpreters in training and working interpreters. Oller (1988) describes the ability to complete linguistic patterns as "active hypothesis testing." Thus, completion involves more than just guessing what would come next in the speech. The interpreter must check the hypothesis against what has already been heard or seen to know whether the hypothesis is a possible and logical direction for the speech to follow. What do you think the speaker is going to say? That helps you form a hypothesis to test. Through careful listening and analysis, you will know whether your hypothesis is being supported by what the speaker says next or whether you need to revise your ideas about what the speaker is planning to say. The completion process also has a retroactive component. Once the active hypothesis has been made, the interpreter checks the continuing message to see whether the hypothesis is supported.

Phrase-level pattern inference requires at least two important skills. First is a good command of ASL and its grammatically acceptable constructions. Second, you will need the ability to logically complete an idea based on the context and the information you have seen up to the point where the phrase ends.

The Role of Phrase-Level Pattern Inference Skills in the Interpreting Process

Well-developed pattern inference skills allow you to hypothesize how a sentence, paragraph, or longer text might logically be completed. This is important because interpreters are usually planning ahead and exploring possible directions that the speaker may take. Pattern inference skills are positively related to world knowledge. The greater your world knowledge and the larger your stores of schemas, or information patterns for how things work, the greater the likelihood that your set of possibilities will contain an appropriate choice. This kind of important information is generally based on prior knowledge. In other words, the more you know about how things work and the more information and knowledge you have, the more likely you will be able to hypothesize logical endings while interpreting. The more practice and awareness you have of the importance of phrase-level pattern inference, the less effort you will need to devote to this aspect of the interpreting process.

In general, it is more likely that pattern inference skills will be accurate if you have already established a schema or general frame of reference for an idea. For example, if a person listening to a mechanic already knows how an automobile engine works, then the person will more likely be able to create predictions that are in line with what the mechanic wants to convey. This does not mean that that interpreters should create their own endings to sentences or stories, but rather that they should use active hypothesis testing to prepare their minds for the probable directions of the speech. Accurate and reliable pattern inference skills will allow greater capacity management during the interpreting process. As noted by Gile (1995), the greater the capacity for the components of the interpreting processes, including pattern inference skills, the more likely that the interpreter will have adequate cognitive capacity to manage the entire simultaneous interpreting processes.

Ability to Tolerate Ambiguity

As an interpreter develops good pattern inference skills, linguistic insight also develops. Insight into how ideas fit together helps interpreters create hypotheses about what the speaker will say. As pattern inference skills develop, it is likely that the interpreter will become more knowledgeable about ambiguity, understanding that various meanings could be intended by the signer. Ambiguity means that a sign or phrase could have more than one meaning. Ideally, the context will allow the interpreter to know which meaning is intended. If not, then the interpreter's heightened sensitivity allows him or her to know that there is more than one possible meaning. If context does not make it clear which meaning is intended and the interpreter is aware of this, the interpreter must stop the speaker to ask for clarification, if at all possible. Some ambiguity must be tolerated as the speaker reveals his or her point. Sometimes the speaker may not show or tell the interpreter how the ideas being presented are related, which can add to the interpreter's cognitive load. Occasionally stopping the speaker for clarification will not reduce the ambiguity for the interpreter or other listeners because there are times when the speaker is unable to clearly make the desired point.

More experienced interpreters generally will be able to tolerate more ambiguity than those who are just learning to interpret. Moser (1997) suggests that one of the most notable differences between novice and expert interpreters is that the novices tend to be distracted by superficial problems along the way and use a more "microview" approach, wherein they can get "lost" in the details. Expert interpreters, on the other hand, tend to use a more global approach, or a "macroview,' which allows them to avoid getting lost in the details and therefore to follow the overall message better. Pattern inference skills help students of interpreting reach that macroview.

Pattern inference skills are also important at the idea level. At the idea level you work to select ideas or concepts that would logically fit in the context. Interpreters often must deal with visual distractions that interfere with comprehension. These distractions can include visual interruptions that override or block out a part of the signed message. For example, if someone walks between you and the signer, you may miss part of what was said because you could not see the signer momentarily. When this happens, it is often possible to continue without stopping the signer. It is likely that the interpreter will be able to "fill in the blank" if good pattern inference skills are in place. Sometimes people are not aware that they have the ability to use pattern inference skills. By practicing drills in this text, you can become more aware of your own pattern inference skills.

In summary, strong pattern inference skills in ASL indicate that signers can make sense of what they are seeing even if they miss a sign or part of a phrase. In general, pattern inference abilities are present for those who have good levels of language proficiency. ASL–English interpreters need high levels of ASL proficiency, so it is important to develop this specific skill.

In Unit 7, two types of exercises are provided. First, pattern inference exercises are provided, followed by comprehension questions. After completing both pattern inference and comprehension, you can return to the pattern inference drills and practice them again. In the pattern inference exercises you will respond by signing a sign or phrase that would make sense. Think of as many different ways to complete the idea as you can. More specific directions are included with each exercise.

PATTERN INFERENCE EXERCISES

EXERCISE 7.1

How to Make a Sandwich

MATT ELLIS

Directions

This exercise has two selections. This short segment allows you to get to know the signer and become accustomed to his signing style and the second segment allows you to focus on pattern inference and comprehension.

Find Exercise 7.1a on your DVD. You will need to record your ASL responses. The selection contains pauses. When the DVD pauses, complete the idea in ASL. Be sure to use ASL syntax and complete the idea logically. The DVD has time built in for your responses but if you need more time, simply pause the DVD yourself. Remember that the goal is to complete the ideas in a way that makes sense. Your response is not wrong if you do not sign exactly what the signer chose to say. This exercise has comprehension questions and study questions. Be sure to respond to them all.

Get to Know the Signer

This short segment allows you to get acquainted with the signer and is about 2 minutes long. Watch the selection and replay it until you can answer the following comprehension questions. Respond in ASL. You do not need to record your responses.

1. Where was he born and raised?

_____

2. Where does he live?

_____

_____

3. Where does he work?

_____

Comprehension Questions

When you have completed the pattern inference exercise, find Exercise 7.1b on your DVD. This version has no pauses. Study it carefully and answer all of the comprehension questions below. Pay particular attention to studying the fingerspelled words. Play each word at least five times in slow motion and study it in context until you are sure you can easily comprehend the finger-spelled word. You should record your ASL responses to the comprehension questions. Be sure to use complete sentences. Then go on to answer the study questions.

1. Study the fingerspelled words. The list shown below provides the English translations of the fingerspelled words. Play the fingerspelled words at least five times until you are sure you can easily recognize each word.

   English Translations of Fingerspelled Words:
   PBJ
   Wheat
   Brand
   Crunchy
   Creamy
   Honey
   Skippy
   Jam
   Strawberry
   Bag

2. What kind of sandwich is he going to explain how to make?

3. What does this sign mean in this context?

02:15:25;00

4. What should you do first?

5. What else should you get?

6. What kind of peanut butter does he like?

7. What else should you get while at the store?

8. What does he caution you to remember to do?

9. How do you begin making the sandwich?

10. How does he like his bread, toasted or not toasted?

11. What do these signs from 02:16:08;14 to 02:16:10;03 mean in this context?

12. What are the next steps in making the sandwich?

13. Which should you use more of, peanut butter or jam?

14. What are the final steps?

Study Questions

1. Watch your recording of your ASL pattern inference. Compare your responses with the way in which the signer actually completed the ideas. In the space provided, note the time codes where the signer used an ASL construction you would like to incorporate into your own signing.

   _____

   _____

2. Practice using the constructions that the signer used and record your work.

3. Turn on your recorder and repeat the exercise, using the new language patterns that you studied in Study Questions 1 and 2.

4. Compare your first and second performance. Did your second performance include more of the constructions that the signer used? Was your ASL intelligible?

5. Using your second recording of your work, study each response and paraphrase it in ASL, remembering to maintain the same meaning as best you can, but using different signs.

EXERCISE 7.2

I'm Deaf Not Blind

ROBERTA GAGE

Directions

This exercise has two selections. The first short segment allows you to get to know the signer and become accustomed to her signing style and the second segment allows you to focus on pattern inference and comprehension.

Find Exercise 7.2a on your DVD. You will need to record your ASL responses. The selection contains pauses. When the DVD pauses, complete the idea in ASL. Be sure to use ASL syntax and complete the idea logically. The DVD has time built in for your responses but if you need more time, simply pause the DVD yourself. Remember that the goal is to complete the ideas in a way that makes sense. Your response is not wrong if you do not sign exactly what the signer chose to say. This exercise has comprehension questions and study questions. Be sure to respond to them all.

Get to Know the Signer

This short segment allows you to get acquainted with the signer and is about 2 minutes long. Watch the selection and replay it until you can answer the following questions. Respond in ASL. You do not need to record your responses.

1. Where did she grow up and where does she live now?

_____

2. Where does she work?

_____

3. What does her job entail?

Comprehension Questions

When you have completed the pattern inference exercise, find Exercise 7.2b on your DVD. This version has no pauses. Study it carefully and answer all of the comprehension questions below. Pay particular attention to studying the fingerspelled words. Play each word at least five times in slow motion and study it in context until you are sure you can easily comprehend the finger-spelled word. You should record your ASL responses to the comprehension questions. Be sure to use complete sentences. Then go on to answer the study questions.

1. Study the fingerspelled words. The list shown below provides the English translations of the fingerspelled words. Play the fingerspelled words at least five times until you are sure you can easily recognize each word.

   ### English Translations of Fingerspelled Words:
   Roberta Gage
   Twin
   Delta
   Braille
   Pissed off
   Cool
   Are

2. Where does the incident take place and who is with Roberta?

3. Where did her father work before retiring and what is the probable connection to this passage?

4. What was the flight attendant's reaction to seeing Roberta and her sister on the flight?

5. What was Roberta's response to the flight attendant leaving without taking her order for a beverage?

6. What did the flight attendant bring back to Roberta's seat?

7. How did Roberta and her sister respond to this?

8. What did her sister request?

9. What did her sister write to the flight attendant?

10. How did the flight attendant respond?

11. What happened next?

Study Questions

1. Watch your recording of your ASL pattern inference. Compare your responses with the way in which the signer actually completed the ideas. In the space provided, note the time codes where the signer used an ASL construction you would like to incorporate into your own signing.

   _____

   _____

2. Practice using the constructions that the signer used and record your work.

3. Turn on your recorder and repeat the exercise, using the new language patterns that you studied in Study Questions 1 and 2.

4. Compare your first and second performances. Did your second performance include more of the constructions that the signer used? Was your ASL intelligible?

5. Using your second recording of your work, study each response and paraphrase it in ASL, remembering to maintain the same meaning as best you can, but using different signs.

EXERCISE 7.3

Room Key

BECKY GAGE

Directions

This exercise has two selections. The first short segment allows you to get to know the signer and become accustomed to her signing style and the second segment allows you to focus on pattern inference and comprehension.

Find Exercise 7.3a on your DVD. You will need to record your ASL responses. The selection contains pauses. When the DVD pauses, complete the idea in ASL. Be sure to use ASL syntax and complete the idea logically. The DVD has time built in for your responses but if you need more time, simply pause the DVD yourself. Remember that the goal is to complete the ideas in a way that makes sense. Your response is not wrong if you do not sign exactly what the signer chose to say. This exercise has comprehension questions and study questions. Be sure to respond to them all.

Get to Know the Signer

This short segment allows you to get acquainted with the signer and is about 2 minutes long. Watch the selection and replay it until you can answer the following questions. Respond in ASL. You do not need to record your responses.

1. Where does she work?

2. How long has she been teaching there?

_____

3. How long has she been teaching altogether?

_____

Comprehension Questions

When you have completed the pattern inference exercise, find Exercise 7.1b on your DVD. This version has no pauses. Study it carefully and answer all of the comprehension questions below. Pay particular attention to studying the fingerspelled words. Play each word at least five times in slow motion and study it in context until you are sure you can easily comprehend the fingerspelled word. You should record your ASL responses to the comprehension questions. Be sure to use complete sentences. Then go on to answer the study questions.

1. Study the fingerspelled words. The list shown below provides the English translations of the fingerspelled words. Play the fingerspelled words at least five times until you are sure you can easily recognize each word.

   ### English Translations of Fingerspelled Words:
   Becky Gage

   Key

   So

2. When does this incident take place?

3. What did the teacher say to her?

4. How did Becky respond to the teacher?

5. Did the teacher believe her?

6. What happened the following week?

7. Why did Becky go to the class that Roberta was attending?

8. What was the teacher's reaction?

Study Questions

1. Watch your recording of your ASL pattern inference. Compare your responses with the way in which the signer actually completed the ideas. In the space provided, note the time codes where the signer used an ASL construction you would like to incorporate into your own signing.

_____

_____

2. Practice using the constructions that the signer used and record your work.

3. Turn on your recorder and repeat the exercise, using the new language patterns that you studied in Study Questions 1 and 2.

4. Compare your first and second performance. Did your second performance include more of the constructions that the signer used? Was your ASL intelligible?

5. Using your second recording of your work, study each response and paraphrase it in ASL, remembering to maintain the same meaning as best you can, but using different signs.

Progress Tracking Sheet

A progress tracking sheet is provided at the end of each unit. This sheet is designed to help you keep track of which exercises you have completed and how well you have done on these exercises. A rating system is presented for you to rate the outcomes of your work on the exercises. After completing each exercise and activity, fill in the tracking sheet. Your instructor may ask you to copy and submit the tracking sheet for each unit. Rate your performance on the exercises using the following scale: excellent (no serious errors) = 5 points; good (some errors, but not serious) = 4 points; fair (many errors, some serious) = 3 points; not satisfactory (many errors, most are serious) = 2 points; poor (missed the point of the exercise—must redo) =1 point.

Exercise Number and Name	Date	First Performance Rating	Second Performance Rating	Questions and Reminders
Exercise 7.1 How to Make a Sandwich				
Exercise 7.2 I'm Not Deaf Blind				
Exercise 7.3 Room Key				

References

Arjona, E. (1984). Education of translators and interpreters. In M. McIntire (Ed.), *New Dialogues in interpreter education. Proceedings of the fourth national Conference of Interpreter Trainers Convention,* (p. 1–36). Silver Spring, MD: Registry of Interpreters for the Deaf.

American Heritage Dictionary of the English Language (3rd ed.). (1992). Boston: Houghton Mifflin.

Atkinson, R. C., & Shiffrin, R. M. (1968). Human memory: A proposed system and its control processes. In K. W. Spence (Ed.), *The psychology of learning and motivation: Advances in research and theory*. New York: Academic Press.

Baddeley, A. (1990). *Human memory: Theory and practice*. Hillsdale, NJ: Erlbaum.

Carroll, R.T. (2005) *What Do You Know about Your Memory?* Retrieved March 26, 2006 , from http://www.aucegypt.edu/academic/interpretings/Memory.html.

Cokely, D. (1986). The effects of time lag on interpreter errors. *Sign Language Studies, 53,* 341–376.

Cokely, D. (1992b). *Interpretation: A sociolinguistic model*. Silver Spring, MD: Linstok.

Dancette, J. (1997). Mapping meaning and comprehension in translation. In J. Danks et al. (Eds.), *Cognitive processes in translation and interpreting* (pp. 77–104). Thousand Oaks, CA: Sage.

Danks, J., et al. (Eds.). (1997). *Cognitive processes in translation and interpreting*. Thousand Oaks, CA: Sage.

Daro, V. & Fabbro. F. (1994). Verbal memory during simultaneous interpretation: Effects of phonological interference. Applied Linguistics 1994 15(4):365–381; Oxford University Press.

DeGroot, A. (1997). The cognitive study of translation and interpretation. In J. Danks et al. (Eds.), *Cognitive processes in translation and interpreting* (pp. 25–57). Thousand Oaks, CA: Sage.

Gerver, D. 1976 Empirical studies of simultaneous interpretation: A review and a model in R. Brislin (Ed.), *Translation*. New York: Gardner Press.

Gile, D. (1995). *Basic concepts and models for interpreter and translator training*. Philadelphia: John Benjamins.

Gile, D. (2005). Theories for Research, Theories for Training. Professional Education of 21 Century Translators and Interpreters Monterey, California, September 9–11, 2005 Graduate School of Translation and Interpretation, Monterey Institute of International Studies

Gonzalez, R., et al. (1991). *Fundamentals in court interpretation: Theory, policy and practice*. Durham, NC: Carolina Academic Press.

Guillory, L. (1966). *Expressive fingerspelling for hearing adults*. Baton Rouge: Claitor's Publishing Division.

Hardyck, C., & Petrinovich, L. F. (1977). Left-handedness. *Psychological Bulletin, 84*, 385–404.

Ingram, R., (1984). Teaching decalage skills. In M. L. McIntire (Ed.), *New dialogues in interpreter education: Proceedings of the Fourth National Conference of Interpreter Trainers Convention* (pp. 291–308). Silver Spring, MD.

Kelly, L. (1979). *The true interpreter: A history of translation theory and practice in the west*. New York: St. Martin's.

Kurz, I. (1992). Shadowing exercises in interpreter training. In C. Dollerup & A. Loddegaard (Eds.), *Teaching translation and interpreting training, talent and experience* (pp. 245–250). Philadelphia: John Benjamins.

Kussmaul, P. (1995). *Training the translator*. Philadelphia: John Benjamins.

Lambert, S. (1989). Plenary session. In S. Wilcox (Ed.), *New dimensions in interpreter education: Evaluation and critique* (pp. 113–125). Conference of Interpreter Trainers.

Lambert, S. (1992). Aptitude testing for simultaneous interpretation at the University of Ottawa. In L. Gran & J. Dodds (Eds.), *The interpreter's newsletter*. Trieste: University of Trieste.

Larson, M. (1984). *Meaning based translation: A guide to cross-language equivalence*. Lanham, MD: University of America.

Longley, P. (1989). The use of aptitude testing in the selection of students for conference interpretation training. In L. Gran & J. Dodds (Eds.), *The theoretical and practical aspects of teaching conference interpretation* (pp. 105–109). Campanotto Editore, Udine.

MacWhinney, B. (1997). *Simultaneous interpretation and the competition model.* In J. Danks et al. (Eds.), Cognitive processes in translation and interpreting (pp. 215–233). Thousand Oaks, CA: Sage.

Moser, B. (1997). Beyond curiosity: Can interpreting research meet the challenge? In J. Danks et al. (Eds.), *Cognitive processes in translation and interpreting* (pp. 176–195). Thousand Oaks, CA: Sage.

Moser–Mercer, B. (1983). Defining aptitude for simultaneous interpretation. In M. L. McIntire (Ed.), *New dialogues in interpreter education: Proceedings of the Fourth National Conference of Interpreter Trainers Convention* (pp. 43–70). Silver Spring, MD: RID Publications.

Moser, B. (1978) Simultaneous interpretation: A hypothetical model and its practical application in D. Gerver & H. Sinaiko (Eds.), *Language, interpretation and communication.* (pp. 353–368). New York: Plenum Press.

Nicodemus, B. (2009). *Prosodic Markers and Utterance Boundaries in American Sign Language Interpretation.* Washington DC: Gallaudet University Press.

Oller, J. (1988). Making sense in interpreter education programs: Evaluation. In S. Wilcox (Ed.), *New dimensions in interpreter education: Evaluation and critique. Proceedings of the Seventh National Convention of the Conference of Interpreter Trainers* (pp. 1–20). Conference of Interpreter Trainers.

Paradis, M., (1994). Toward a neurolinguistic theory of simultaneous translation: The framework. International journal of psycholinguistics. 9(2), 133–145

Patrie, C. (1997). *Fingerspelled Names and Introductions: A template building approach.* San Diego, CA: DawnSignPress

Patrie, C. (1995). *The readiness-to-work gap.* In E. Winston (Ed.), Mapping our course: A collaborative venture. Proceedings of the 1944 Conference of Interpreter Trainers Convention (pp.53–55). Conference of Interpreter Trainers.

Patrie, Carol. (1992) "Theoretical issues in fingerspelled word recognition"". *Journal of Interpretation,* (pp. 51–91) Silver Spring, MD: Registry of Interpreters for the Deaf.

Peterson, L. R., & Peterson, M. J. (1959) *Short-term retention of individual verbal items.* Journal of Experimental Psychology, 10, 12–21.

Sandler, W., & Lillo-Martin, D. (2001). *Natural sign languages.* In M. Aronoff & J. Rees-Miller (Eds.), The handbook of linguistics (pp. 533–562). Malden, MA: Blackwell Publishers.

Schweda Nicholson, N. (1996). Perspectives on the role of memory in interpretation: A critical review of recent literature. In M. Jerome-O'Keefe (Ed.), *Global vision: Proceedings of the 37th Annual Conference of the American*

Translators Association (pp. 99–113). Alexandria, VA: American Translator's Association.

Seal, B. (1999). Educational interpreters document efforts to improve. *VIEWS,* 16(2), 14.

Sperling, G. (1960). The information available in brief visual presentations. *Psychological Monographs,* 74 (11, Whole No. 498).

Sunnari, M. (1995). Processing strategies in simultaneous interpreting: Experts vs. novices. In C. Nixon (Ed.), *Connections: Proceedings of the 36th Annual Conference of the American Translators Association* (pp. 157–165). Alexandria, VA: American Translator's Association.

Taylor, M. (2002). *Interpretation skills: American Sign Language to English.* Edmonton: Interpreting Consolidated.

Tulvig, E. (1983). *Elements of episodic memory.* Oxford: Oxford University Press.

Waugh, N. C. and Norman, D. A. (1965). Primary Memory. *Psychological Review* 72 (2), 89–104.

Zakia, R. and R. Haber (1971). Sequential letter and word recognition in deaf and hearing subjects. Perception and Psychophysicis. 9:110–114.